DATE DUE

Guerrillas in the 1960's

PRINCETON STUDIES IN WORLD POLITICS

Number 1

PRINCETON STUDIES IN WORLD POLITICS

1. Guerrillas in the 1960's
   Peter Paret and John W. Shy

2. A Theory of Foreign Policy
   George Modelski

3. Limited Strategic War
   Edited by Klaus Knorr and Thornton Read

Guerrillas in the 1960's

PETER PARET and JOHN W. SHY

Second Edition

Published for the Center of International Studies
Princeton University

by

FREDERICK A. PRAEGER, *Publisher*

New York

BOOKS THAT MATTER

Published in the United States of America in 1962 by
Frederick A. Praeger, Inc., Publisher
64 University Place, New York 3, N.Y.

Second edition, 1962

All rights reserved

© 1962 by Frederick A. Praeger, Inc.
Library of Congress Catalog Card Number: 62-17978

To

B. H. LIDDELL HART

Preface to the Second Edition

Since the summer of 1961, when our original manuscript was completed, guerrilla warfare has lost none of its actual and potential significance. In the intervening period, its obvious importance as a technique of international violence has led to the publication of numerous studies on the subject. Nevertheless, there still seems to be a need to identify and to analyze as concisely as possible the elements that make up guerrilla warfare, and to consider their bearing on American policy.

With the exception of a few minor changes, the main body of the text has been left untouched for the second edition. The Introduction has, however, been recast, and we have expanded the final chapter. The number of titles in the bibliography has been nearly doubled.

In the course of writing, we have benefited from numerous comments and suggestions. We owe particular gratitude to Mr. Charles MacArthur Carman, Jr., Mr. Frank Wisner II, Professor S. M. Chiu, Lieutenant Colonel T. N. Greene of the *Marine Corps Gazette*, Professor Morton Kaplan, and to our colleagues Professors Klaus Knorr, Raymond Grew, and Davis Bobrow.

Princeton, N.J.
March, 1962

Contents

I   INTRODUCTION   3

II   THE DEFENSIVE FUNCTION OF GUERRILLA
WARFARE   6

    Early Historical Experiences   6

    Clausewitz' Analysis   11

III   THE INSURRECTIONARY AND OFFENSIVE
FUNCTION   16

    Communism and Insurrection   18

    The Integration of Political and Military
Leadership   21

    The Evolution of Guerrilla Theory   24

IV   GUERRILLAS AND COUNTERGUERRILLAS   31

    Guevara and the Dilemmas of the Guerrilla Leader   31

    The Tasks of Counterguerrilla Action   40

V   GUERRILLAS AND AMERICAN POLICY   52

    Defensive Use of Guerrillas   53

    Defense Against Guerrillas   59

    Offensive Use of Guerrillas   63

    Conclusion   69

A SELECTED BIBLIOGRAPHY   85

Guerrillas in the 1960's

I

Introduction

A new dimension was added to American military policy during the first year of the Kennedy Administration. In the preceding decade, the Korean War had broken up the monism of nuclear retaliation and added limited conventional war to our strategic doctrine. Much in the same way, in 1961, the Cuban revolution combined with the deteriorating Western position in Southeast Asia to shift attention to what was variously called guerrilla, subversive, sublimited, brushfire, and unconventional warfare.

In April, 1961, the Secretary of Defense asked for a "150 per cent increase in the size of antiguerrilla forces."[1] The following month, in an address to Congress, President Kennedy emphasized "the orientation of existing forces for the conduct of non-nuclear war, paramilitary operations and sublimited, or unconventional wars." He went on to announce that American "special forces and unconventional forces will be increased and reori-

[1] *New York Times,* April 25, 1961.

ented."[2] The refinement of training and the elaboration of policy kept pace with the build-up of men and matériel.[3] General William B. Rosson's appointment, in February, 1962, to the new post of Special Assistant to the Chief of Staff for Special Warfare provided further indication that a new weapons system was in the making.

This development received a generally enthusiastic welcome. But in the nation's readiness to underwrite methods of unconventional warfare, some essential distinctions were overlooked or became muddled. The confusion was particularly noticeable in the press and in Congress: The woods-ranging sharpshooter of American tradition was once again invoked, the differences between fighting against guerrillas and fighting as guerrillas were obscured, and the political implications of a highly political kind of fighting were largely ignored. From the Administration itself came strong hints that guerrillas might prove to be the means of overthrowing Communist regimes.[4]

Uncritical enthusiasm for the newest miracle weapon has now subsided. Confusion and vague optimism lessened as the general problem of unconventional warfare was seen more and more in terms of specific situations—

[2] *New York Times,* May 26, 1961.

[3] Compare, for example, the greatly revised and expanded 1961 Army field manuals on unconventional warfare with their 1958 predecessors.

[4] See, for instance, the statement by Lieutenant General A. G. Trudeau, Chief of Research and Development, U.S. Army, in the *New York Herald Tribune,* April 10, 1961.

in terms of South Vietnam, for instance. But although there was increasing sophistication, which led to useful action, much uncertainty and disagreement continued among the various departments and agencies of the government charged with formulating and implementing unconventional-warfare policies. In this realm of political and military strategy, a coherent doctrine, as well as genuine coordination in carrying it out, has yet to emerge.

This book attempts to dispel some of the confusion by analyzing the major military component of unconventional warfare—the guerrilla. The historical approach is particularly useful here, for in no other form of conflict has the human factor been affected so little by developments in military technology. Changes in purpose and methods have, however, proved of the greatest significance; they need spelling out, but they too can be properly understood only by tracing them to their roots. Today's pervasive concern with Communism, which tends to distort analysis of every international problem, is best mitigated by studying both what is new and what is timeless in contemporary irregular warfare. Once we have understood how the guerrilla fought and what he achieved in the past, once we know his strengths and his limitations, we will be better able to estimate what he can achieve today and in the future.

II

The Defensive Function of Guerrilla Warfare

EARLY HISTORICAL EXPERIENCES

Spanish resistance to Napoleonic invasion put the word "guerrilla" into the dictionary, but civilians taking up arms and fighting as irregulars are as old as war. Caesar, for one, encountered them in Gaul and Germany, and in succeeding centuries, their formations and tactics frequently played a part in European conflicts. Their potential increased with the expansion of war in the last years of the eighteenth century. Spain's struggle against the French not only gave the irregular fighter a new name but also provided an early case study of one type of modern guerrilla warfare. An understanding of why and how Spaniards fought between 1808 and 1813 is essential since this struggle embodied basic characteristics that apply to later times and places.

Above all, Spaniards were willing to fight. Many other European peoples who in large part regarded their own

6

governments with apathy or hostility, and who welcomed the message of the French Revolution brought to them by the Napoleonic armies, lacked sufficient motives for resistance. But in Spain, conditions were right for violence from the beginning. Spanish peasants, influenced by their priests and nobles, had always hated foreigners, felt some attachment to the monarchy, which Napoleon had overthrown, and now feared the destruction of the Spanish Church. These feelings, not the externally imposed discipline of a regular army, held the Spanish guerrillas together and made them willing to risk death.

The guerrillas fought to protect their lands and their way of life; their objective was defensive. But they could hardly hope to expel or annihilate what was then the best army in Europe. Whenever the French were willing to allot sufficient forces and take the necessary casualties, they could sweep a limited area clean of opposition and effectively control it. The Spanish objective was thus not only defensive, it was also by necessity psychological. The strategic task of the guerrillas was not to destroy the French but to undermine their will to stay in the country.

While both the impetus and objective of Spanish guerrilla action lay in the realms of ideology and morale, a third determining factor was geographical. The guerrillas based themselves in mountainous, inaccessible terrain that only they knew well. The road net, poor even

7

by the standards of a century and a half ago, channeled French movements narrowly, provided critical targets for attack, and rendered surprise or encirclement of the guerrillas almost out of the question. A well-functioning intelligence system might have made up for the French army's geographic handicap, but the patriotic basis of the conflict blocked its access to local sources of information.

Clearly, the Spanish capacity for guerrilla war was very high. Of almost equal significance in the conflict were certain French weaknesses. The very qualities that had made the French successful against other regular armies rendered them vulnerable to irregular attack. The Revolution had produced military leaders who stressed audacity and speed of movement, usually at the cost of security. Mobility was further increased by the French system of requisitions and living off the country, which freed units from the fixed supply-point system of the past. But in Spain these innovations worked against them. Neglected flanks and rear proved natural areas for irregular operations, as they still are today. Stragglers, foraging parties, and detached units provided easy targets for guerrilla attack. Improvised supply made the French extremely dependent on the natives, and their requisitions upon the already poverty-stricken country fanned the hatred that had initially aroused the peasants and villagers to fight. As modern irregulars can exploit the weaknesses of mechanized units organized and equipped to develop the greatest possible forward thrust, so the Spanish exploited the tactical and logistical limitations of the French.

Finally, Spanish resistance was marked by a fact that has been too frequently overlooked: Spaniards used irregular tactics only after their regular forces had collapsed. Guerrilla strategy was not the preferred strategy; it was the only strategy that remained available. Moreover, it did not succeed until a British army entered Spain from Portugal. In Spain, as throughout history, guerrilla warfare was the weapon of the militarily weak.

It is not difficult to illustrate this basic characteristic of the guerrilla. Despite the extraordinary potential of armed civilians at the disposal of the American colonies, General Washington and the Continental Congress rejected a partisan strategy as long as there were other choices. Instead, they concentrated on building a regular army. Only after the defeat of part of that force and its militia auxiliaries in the South did the American revolutionaries adopt guerrilla warfare.

Similarly, the Boers in South Africa resorted to guerrilla warfare only after they had been defeated in open battle. True, in North America as in South Africa, the British had great trouble in coping with guerrilla forces. But American colonists and Boer farmers were not simply being dull-witted when they refused to depend on this type of warfare until all else had failed. On the contrary. They knew the price of guerrilla operations and were reluctant to pay it.

Civil War historians have lavished praise on John Mosby for his leadership of Confederate irregulars in northwestern Virginia, but they have failed to consider the eventual consequences of his little guerrilla war. No one doubts Mosby's skill in making Union operations in this area very difficult, but in 1864, Sheridan devastated the Shenandoah Valley, and systematically and successfully destroyed the guerrillas' base. Sheridan's counterstrategy was ruthless and effective, and it demonstrates some of the special costs of resorting to guerrilla warfare.

Not only must the irregular fighters themselves be able to bear the extraordinary physical and psychic burdens of animal-like existence,[1] they must also be prepared to see great injury done to the society they strive to defend. Used against a strong and determined opponent, guerrilla warfare is sure to result in heavy damage to people and property, and to exert severe strain on the political and social structure. From the commander's point of view, moreover, there are grave risks involved in basing his plans on precarious civilian attitudes, especially when his strategy is one of attrition, which requires considerable, perhaps intolerable, time to do its

[1] For a graphic account of what one partisan force suffered in a short period, see Sir Fitzroy Maclean, *Disputed Barricade* (London, 1957).

work. Finally, there can be little assurance that it will
work; even victorious guerrilla leaders have rarely
argued that guerrilla operations can succeed without the
eventual aid of regular forces.

CLAUSEWITZ' ANALYSIS

The first serious attempt to synthesize the characteristics of irregular operations and to define their role in
warfare, once it had broken through the net of eight-
eenth-century conventions and limitations, was undertaken by Clausewitz. The section on defense in his work
On War includes a chapter on military action of the
civilian population.[2] Since, directly or indirectly, it provided the basis for most subsequent theories of irregular
warfare, the chapter deserves to be quoted at some
length. In Europe, Clausewitz begins, popular war "is a
phenomenon of the nineteenth century. It has its advocates and its opponents; the latter either for political
reasons, since they consider such a war a revolutionary
method, a state of anarchy declared lawful, as dangerous

2 Book VI, chap. 26. The German title of the chapter, *"Volksbewaff-
nung"* ("Arming the People"), is rendered in the standard English edition by O. S. Matthijs Jolles (Washington, D.C., 1950), as "Arming the
Nation." Although at the time Clausewitz wrote, the difference in meaning between "people" and "nation" remained somewhat ambiguous, it
nevertheless existed. Besides, Clausewitz makes it plain that by *Volks-
bewaffnung* he means something beyond conscription and militia, i.e.,
the arming of civilians, who operate in irregular formations. The quotations from *On War* in the text have been newly translated by the
present authors.

to internal social order as it is to the enemy, or on military grounds, since they believe the result is not commensurate with the expenditure of effort."

Clausewitz intentionally leaves aside the political problems created by arming civilians. His discussion treats popular war solely on its operational merits, as a means of fighting. To the objection that conventional military methods are a more rational use of a nation's resources, he replies with obvious and conscious exaggeration that a country's ideological potential is tapped only in popular wars. He then spells out the principles and the efficacy of popular resistance.

It is unsuited to major actions, "whose effect is concentrated in time and space. Like the process of evaporation in nature, its effect depends on the extent of its surface. The greater this is, and the greater its contact with the opposing army—in other words, the more the enemy extends himself—the greater is the effect of an armed populace. Like a slow, gradual fire it destroys the bases of the enemy force." To be sure, irregular operations do not inevitably lead to victory; even if they are successful, they require much time to reach a point of culmination, and they can rarely do it without assistance. "For this crisis to be produced by popular action alone presupposes either an invaded area greater than that of any European country except Russia, or a degree of disproportion between the invader and the size of the country that does not occur in reality. Unless we wish to chase a mirage, we must conceive of the people's war in coordination with operations carried out by a regular army, both acting according to an over-all plan."

Clausewitz lists five general conditions for the successful pursuit of guerrilla warfare:

1. The war must be carried on in the interior of the country.
2. The war cannot hinge on a single battle.
3. The theater of war must extend over a considerable area.
4. The national character must support the war.
5. The country must be irregular, difficult, inaccessible.

Clausewitz then rapidly sketches the operational limitations of the guerrilla: "Militia and armed civilians cannot and should not be employed against the main force of the enemy, or even against sizable units. They should not try to crack the core, but only nibble along the surface and on the edges. They should rise in provinces lying to one side of the main theater of war, which the invader does not enter in force, in order to draw these areas entirely from his grasp. These storm clouds forming on his flanks should also follow to the rear of his advance. . . . The enemy has no other means with which to oppose the actions of armed civilians than the dispatching of numerous detachments to escort his convoys, to occupy posts, defiles, bridges, etc. Just as the first efforts of the people will be insignificant, so these detachments will be weak, because he is afraid of dividing his forces too much. It is on these small units that the spark of popular war really catches fire; at some points, the enemy is overpowered by sheer numbers, courage and enthusiasm grow, and the intensity of the struggle increases until the culmination comes, which will decide the entire issue."

The psychological and organizational characteristics of armed civilian groups suggest to Clausewitz that although they form a weapon of strategic defense, they generally or even always must be tactically on the offensive. Their offensive actions should be made up of pinpricks, raids, ambushes; although a favorable position should be defended, it is still preferable to break off the engagement and scatter, or withdraw for a subsequent counterattack, than to make a last-ditch stand. As Mao Tse-tung was to write a century later, "The ability to run away is the very characteristic of the guerrilla."[3] Only rarely should civilian levies concentrate in mass and take the risks of being destroyed at one blow.

Clausewitz' short chapter on arming the people remained a rough draft that never received the revisions he intended to make in it. Despite the idealistic, some-

[3] *Strategic Problems in the Anti-Japanese Guerrilla War* (Peking, 1960), p. 15. See the slightly different translation in *The Selected Works of Mao Tse-tung* (London, 1954), II, 128.

what metaphysical strain of the text, he caught the essence of guerrilla warfare as it appeared in the years between Valmy and Waterloo, and defined the military and psychological characteristics of the patriotic volunteer defending his homeland, either spontaneously or in officially organized formations, but always employing irregular tactics.

III

The Insurrectionary and
Offensive Function

The employment of guerrillas against a foreign invader is well established in military history and theory, and certainly remains conceivable today and in the future. In the last two centuries, however, two further uses of the guerrilla have clearly emerged: he may be a weapon of insurrection, and he may be the agent of foreign aggression.

In the past, people rising against an oppressive government often fought as guerrillas. This is natural enough, since terror, bushwhacking, and small raids are the only military means readily available to civilians. The modern prototypes of insurgent guerrilla operations, however, stem from the age of the French Revolution. Fifteen years before the Spanish peasants took up arms against Napoleon, the young French Republic had to contend with a whole series of counterrevolutionary outbreaks that, by the use of irregular military tactics, combined with propaganda and foreign support, attempted to re-establish the Bourbon monarchy.[1] But only in our time has guerrilla action become systematized as a weapon of the disaffected for the seizure of power. The great Communist instances are the Russian Revolution and Mao's conquest of China. Among the successful non-Communist examples may be mentioned the Arab revolt, with T. E. Lawrence's guerrilla campaign against Turkish communications; the Jewish operations against the British and Arabs between 1945 and the founding of Israel; and EOKA's fight to gain Cyprus' independence from the United Kingdom.

The third use of the guerrilla—that of fighting in his native country as an agent of a foreign power—is more difficult to pin down. This may seem surprising, since Communist agitation and subversion are well-known facts of contemporary life. But until today, the Communists have never organized and dominated a foreign guerrilla movement from the outset. It most nearly happened in Indochina, where the rebel Vietminh were trained in China and equipped by the Chinese very early in the game. Yet it would be a mistake to see the French defeat simply as the outcome of an externally manipulated attack. As an observer pointed out at the time, "The French have never encouraged, or even allowed,

[1] For a recent study of the most important popular rising against the Republic, see Peter Paret, *Internal War and Pacification: The Vendée, 1789–1796* (Research Monograph No. 12, Center of International Studies, Princeton University [1961]).

any moderate constitutional party comparable to the Indian Congress Party to exist; hence the Communist Party had absorbed nationalist aspirations without competition. . . . Ho Chi Minh has a stronger position in Southeast Asia than any of the other Communist leaders because he gained strength in a period when he was the incarnation of nationalism and when there was no alternative to him."[2] Here, too, though the guerrillas clearly helped advance the interests of a foreign power and received its active support, their basic strength derived from identifying with their own compatriots. If a sufficient number of Indochinese had not wanted a greater measure of independence from France, if they had not been disgusted with corrupt puppet regimes, externally manipulated agents would never have got beyond the stage of banditry.

COMMUNISM AND INSURRECTION

Though Communism has learned to exploit people's desires for independence and economic improvement, it does not hold a monopoly on the use of guerrillas as tools of insurrection or as agents of a foreign power, nor did it originate these uses. Rather, as has already been suggested, these are products of the modern age, when, in Clausewitz' words, war was taken out of the hands of

[2] Edward L. Katzenbach, Jr., "Indo-China: A Military-Political Appreciation," *World Politics,* IV (January, 1952), 205.

small groups of professionals and "again became a matter for the people as a whole."[3]

Since the eighteenth century, war has grown progressively more encompassing. The Industrial Revolution, first in the West and then in the whole world, and the simultaneous acceleration of nationalism and the development of the modern state have created new means and new motives for armed conflict. Once war breaks out, all aspects of national life are caught up in it, each affecting the others. In particular—although until recently governments and general staffs have found great difficulty accepting this—there remains almost no area that may be termed purely military or exclusively political.

A full understanding of Clausewitz' famous dictum on the interaction of war and politics is the key to successful modern guerrilla operations. The guerrillas' motive for fighting is at least partly political—or, to put it differently, ideological. They are enrolled not only by administrative machinery, but also by some powerful idea —love of country, hatred of the foreigner, envy of the rich landowner. Social pressure, at times even terror, plays a role; but it requires an element of individual conviction to compel men to take part in this most punishing kind of combat. Undoubtedly, this conviction can be created; yet even sophisticated processes of in-

[3] *Op. cit.*, Book VIII, chap. 3b.

doctrination are ineffective unless they can exploit real problems, real hopes and fears.

In mobilizing people for irregular warfare, Marxists perhaps derive an advantage from their philosophy. In terms of Communist theory, the overlapping of politics and war makes sense. It makes sense in the conflicts between sovereign states; it makes even more sense in revolutions and internal wars. To the traditional motives for popular action—patriotism and self-interest—Communism has joined an aggressive supranational political theory incorporating a view of history that claims inevitable success for its policies. The combination provides popular discontent the world over with an effective and flexible ideological framework for violent action.

In the long run, however, it is not obedience to an abstract ideological doctrine but the practical understanding of the relation between war and politics that pays off. As Mao, the most successful modern practitioner of guerrilla warfare, has written: "Without a political goal, guerrilla warfare must fail, as it must if its political objectives do not coincide with the aspirations of the people. . . ."[4] Or, as an Algerian nationalist recently stated, "[Military] strength exists when the masses are mobilized and penetrated by ideas . . . it is impossible to win the other battles if the ideological

[4] *Mao Tse-tung on Guerrilla Warfare,* trans. Brigadier General Samuel B. Griffith (New York, 1961), p. 43.

battle with the people has not been won . . . the ideological situation at the lower levels must be known."[5]

THE INTEGRATION OF POLITICAL AND MILITARY LEADERSHIP

Political factors impinge as directly on the actual operations of irregular warfare. This may hold true even at a low tactical level. For example, although an attack on an enemy strong point may seem desirable, it may alienate the local inhabitants or expose them to reprisals against which they cannot be protected. Since the good will of the population is essential for the irregular fighter, the political implications may well outweigh the possible military gain and dictate the cancellation of the raid.

It is to be noted that modern revolutionary movements, be they Communist, Fascist, or simply nationalist, have always clearly understood the need to integrate political and military leadership in their combat units. The Russian and satellite political commissars are well-known examples. Up to the final weeks of World War II, the National Socialists strove to enlarge the functions of the party's representatives at the front, the *NS-Führungsoffiziere.*[6] Among the most extreme

[5] Abdel Kader Chanderli, Permanent Representative of the Front of National Liberation (FLN), interview, March 2 and 3, 1961.

[6] See the documentary publication by Waldemar Besson, "Zur Geschichte des nationalsozialistischen Führungsoffiziers," in *Vierteljahrshefte für Zeitgeschichte,* IX (January, 1961).

solutions has been that of the Algerian rebels, whose tactical formations down to the section have a politico-military commander, who is assisted by a staff of three subordinates responsible for political affairs, military affairs, liaison and intelligence. The politico-military hierarchy is based on a territorial organization, a colonel, for example, being the supreme authority in each *wilaya* (region). The typical command structure of a region takes the form shown on the opposite page.[7]

As can be seen, four lines of authority and responsibility exist. Of these, two—the over-all commanders and their liaison and intelligence officers—cover both the political and military areas, the third is exclusively political, the fourth exclusively military. The two realms, it has been pointed out, are in effect evenly balanced.[8]

Certainly, the political officers help to establish and retain control over forces that are potentially dangerous to the civilian leadership. But it would be wrong to see their functions only in this light. Their presence with the troops constitutes a recognition that political problems are part of all combat operations, and that enthusiasm and fanaticism among the soldiers aid military effectiveness. The maintenance of ideological solidarity, which in authoritarian movements can be awakened and

---

7 J. Perret-Gentil, "L'Armée française face à la guerre subversive: II. La technique et les procédés de la rebellion organisée en Algérie," *L'Armée—La Nation*, XIII (November, 1959), 24–26. The ranks of the commands may vary.

8 *Ibid.*, p. 25.

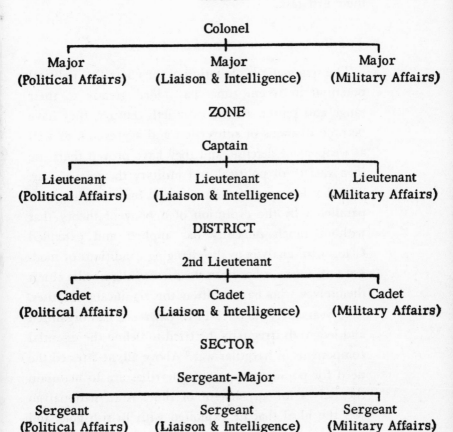

REGION

Colonel

| Major
(Political Affairs) | Major
(Liaison & Intelligence) | Major
(Military Affairs) |

ZONE

Captain

| Lieutenant
(Political Affairs) | Lieutenant
(Liaison & Intelligence) | Lieutenant
(Military Affairs) |

DISTRICT

2nd Lieutenant

| Cadet
(Political Affairs) | Cadet
(Liaison & Intelligence) | Cadet
(Military Affairs) |

SECTOR

Sergeant-Major

| Sergeant
(Political Affairs) | Sergeant
(Liaison & Intelligence) | Sergeant
(Military Affairs) |

effectively channeled without doing violence to the cause represented, has in some instances come to be their first task.

THE EVOLUTION OF GUERRILLA THEORY

The systematic exploitation of the guerrillas' political potential in recent times has added greatly to their range and power. In the twentieth century, they have become weapons of subversion and aggression, as well as weapons of defense, and they have proved their use in a variety of political and military theaters of war. The development of their strategic functions has been paralleled by the evolution of a body of theory that without much difficulty has applied and extended Clausewitz' analysis to the changing conditions of modern war. Often it has been the successful guerrilla chiefs themselves who have written the significant treatises. Two years after Colonel T. E. Lawrence had organized and led Arab irregulars, he tried to define the essential components of irregular war.[9] Above all, he stressed the need for popular support if guerrillas are to maintain themselves for any length of time. Arab nationalism was the ideal that he exploited with British gold and a profound understanding of the tribesmen's psychology. He also understood that his numerically weak forces,

[9] See especially his "The Evolution of a Revolt," which first appeared in *The Army Quarterly*, XLI (October, 1920), and was reprinted in his *Oriental Assembly* (London, 1939).

operating in the vast spaces of the Arabian desert, had to choose objectives other than those pursued on the Western Front. Unable to destroy outright the ability of the enemy to wage war, Arab guerrillas instead had to harass, confuse, exhaust, isolate, and discredit their opponents. In short, Lawrence's strategy is summed up in Clausewitz' image of the flickering, insubstantial, gradually consuming fire, and in B. H. Liddell Hart's concept of the indirect approach. No doubt, Lawrence claimed too much for his guerrillas; they were, in fact, little more than auxiliaries of the Anglo-Indian force under General Allenby. But his campaigns and his writings mark the advent of the guerrilla leader-theorist, consciously, imaginatively, and systematically employing an unorthodox military weapon.

In the Russian Revolution, Lenin and Trotsky did not use guerrillas at the outset. Their capture of political power in the cities and the subversion of the army constituted the immediately decisive actions. During the civil wars that followed, guerrillas cooperated with regular units in defending and securing the Red take-over. But anti-Communist irregulars, representing regional nationalism in such areas as the Ukraine, were of at least equal significance. Perhaps to stress the importance of the industrial workers, the original official history of the Russian Revolution (now withdrawn) makes plain that in the over-all picture Communist guerrillas played only an auxiliary role.

The Communist conquest of China, on the contrary, included periods when peasant guerrillas bore the brunt of the fighting. During the 1920's and early 1930's, irregular operations made up the principal form of Red military action. As the Communists consolidated their position, they turned to more conventional operations, in which guerrillas remained an essential, perhaps even the main, component. When a united front against the Japanese was formed in 1937, Communist regular forces again reverted to guerrilla operations whose strategic functions were at once military and political. By harassing the invader's flanks and rear, they lifted pressure from the Chinese regular armies and wore down Japanese strength and authority. By taking over towns and rural areas, they were able to gain physical and ideological control of increasing numbers of the population.

Winning the support of the population was considered a major objective by the Communists. They attained this objective through a long-term program that combined force with persuasion. Throughout a town or province, a network of agents and propagandists was patiently built up, society was infiltrated by Communist ideas and leaders, at a later stage social pressure or even terror might be used, military successes contributed, and eventually the area would fall under ideological control. For the purpose of conquering China, civilian indoctrination did not have to be either total or very profound. As long as an elite was won over and the majority of the people maintained a benevolent passivity, all strategic and tactical requirements were fulfilled.

Why were the Communist Chinese irregulars on the whole more effective than the better-equipped, conventionally organized divisions of the Japanese and the Kuomintang? The answers lie in the Communists' superior leadership, their numerical strength, the mental block that often afflicts conventional commands when faced by irregulars, the Communist alliance with significant popular causes—nationalism and land reform—and finally the high degree of indoctrination and discipline to which guerrilla officers and men were subjected. Throughout the fighting, the Communist Party operated a political-control apparatus that paid as much attention to shaping and guiding the attitudes of the soldiers as it did to winning the support of the civilian population. The "Three Disciplinary Rules" and the "Eight Points of Attention," which Mao formulated as early as 1928, made it plain to all soldiers that they were expected to behave not as conquerors or bandits, but as the disciplined representatives of a new social and economic order.[10]

[10] For a discussion of the "Three Rules" and "Eight Points," see S. M. Chiu, *Chinese Communist Revolutionary Strategy, 1945–1949: Extracts from Volume IV of Mao Tse-tung's Selected Works* (Research Monograph No. 13, Center of International Studies, Princeton University [1961]).

The third strategic role of the Chinese guerrillas was to provide the experienced manpower with which to build up regular formations when the time came to change retreat and defensive operations into stalemate, and then into counteroffensives. Other Asian and African anticolonial movements have taken over this function as standard doctrine. For example, the Indonesian General Staff history of the war against the Dutch declares that the final aim of guerrilla operations must be the establishment of regular forces. Not that this transformation always proved an easy task in China. The Communist high command, Mao writes, "had to combat the right-wing tendency of localism and guerrillaism, which consists in cherishing guerrilla ways and refusing to turn toward regularization."[11] In the final stage of the Communist conquest, which ended with Chiang's expulsion from the mainland, guerrillas played no more than a secondary role.

A determining factor in Arab, Russian, and Chinese guerrilla warfare—which also applied to Russian partisan operations during World War II—was the nearly unlimited space available. Gradually, as the enemy's lines extended, he grew more vulnerable to attrition and attack. In such theaters of war, guerrillas traded ground for time. Indeed, Mao declared that since

[11] "Problems of War and Strategy," *The Selected Works of Mao Tsetung*, II, 276. The translation, which is somewhat awkward, has been altered slightly for the sake of clarity.

guerrilla warfare requires space for maneuvering, it would not be feasible in a small country such as Belgium.[12] But the Chinese experience must not be turned into a universal law. Geographic limitations can be compensated for by the existence of an inviolable foreign base, which provides equipment and diplomatic support. With Mao at his back, Ho Chi Minh found it possible to adapt Chinese techniques of irregular warfare to the very different and more restricted terrain of Indochina. Greek ideological and diplomatic support enabled the Cypriots to pursue their struggle for years on an island considerably smaller than Connecticut.

EOKA never engaged in large-scale guerrilla warfare. Terror, coupled with the threat of more extensive operations, was sufficient against an opponent who was not willing to wage all-out war. EOKA's objectives were the maintenance of such a degree of insecurity on the island, and the creation of such diplomatic embarrassment for the United Kingdom, that a political settlement would become desirable.

Aside from the limitation of military activity, the Cyprus emergency contained the characteristic features of guerrilla warfare. The partisans represented, exploited, and fought for a popular cause. The Greek population provided the necessary cover and concealment for the guerrillas, who attempted to control the

12 "Strategic Problems in the Anti-Japanese Guerrilla War," *The Selected Works of Mao Tse-tung*, II, 142.

civilians through propaganda, social pressure, and terror. The British forces were faced with the usual difficulties of antiguerrilla operations. Constant disorder and insecurity put their own authority in doubt. The population's fear or antagonism made the collection of information difficult. The frequent impossibility of distinguishing between terrorists and peaceful villagers led to inevitable brutality and injustice on the part of the police and troops, which in turn alienated the people still further.

IV

Guerrillas and Counterguerrillas

GUEVARA AND THE DILEMMAS
OF THE GUERRILLA LEADER

The Castro revolution has produced the latest theorist
of guerrilla warfare, Ernesto (Che) Guevara. The principles stated in his *La Guerra de Guerrillas* are interest-
ing though hardly original; they are timeless tactical
truths understood by all successful guerrilla leaders.[1]
But Guevara does demonstrate how these principles
were adapted to Cuban conditions. Of greater interest
is that he suggests, perhaps unwittingly, some inherent
weaknesses or limitations in irregular warfare—they may
be called the dilemmas of the guerrilla leader—limitations not well understood by either guerrilla or regular.
These dilemmas narrow the area where successful action
is possible and, under some circumstances, may eliminate it altogether.

[1] Our quotations are from a translation prepared for the Department
of the Army and from *Che Guevara on Guerrilla Warfare* (New York,
1961). Condensed translations previously published have important
omissions.

31

In accord with Clausewitz and Mao, Guevara declares that the guerrilla leader must be continually aggressive but must never risk defeat. Defeat not only hurts his small, poorly equipped forces but also carries the special penalty of weakening his hold on the minds of his supporters, both fighters and civilians. But a guerrilla leader who allows offensive activity to slacken likewise runs the risk of weakening confidence and morale, as well as giving his opponent the chance to regain the military initiative.

Second, guerrillas are most secure in comparatively difficult terrain, but in such areas, they rarely find ample supplies, profitable targets, and the civilian leaders who must be won over to their cause. Even the rural regions, the proper political and military base for a guerrilla movement, often comprise what Guevara calls "unfavorable terrain" for irregular operations. He recognizes, indeed, that the most sensitive sections of a country are its areas of highest population density, and that these must be the eventual objective of guerrilla attack and indocrination. But he admits that operations in these areas are extremely dangerous, perhaps impossible except in the form of sporadic terrorism and sabotage, and may cost more than they are worth.

Guevara agrees with most other writers on guerrilla warfare when he asserts that partisans fight not because they are forced to but because they want to. This, however, does not blind him to the extraordinary physical

32

and emotional demands placed upon the irregular fighter, and the fact that guerrilla discipline must be extremely severe. In Cuba, one method of solving this conflict between ideological motive and discipline was to entrust certain judicial functions to "committee[s] chosen from the most meritorious revolutionaries." Nevertheless, such self-imposed discipline cannot tolerate any chinks in the ideological armor and cannot long survive any weakening of motive.

If the guerrilla leader can negotiate the dilemmas presented by the need to be active without being defeated, by terrain and targets, and by desire and discipline, he faces a further dilemma in dealing with the civilian population. It may be taken for granted that in the underdeveloped countries of the world, large parts of the population are dissatisfied with their social and economic lot, but that is not the same thing as supporting guerrilla warfare. Generally, such support is won by political persuasion and maintained by military success. It may also be necessary to use coercion. The question then arises whether coercion will intimidate or alienate the civilian population.

Obviously it will do both; the crucial question is which will preponderate. Guevara is not altogether clear on this point, although he returns to it repeatedly. He admits that when early sympathizers with the guerrillas begin to have second thoughts, "treason" must be "justly punished." Attacking guerrillas display "absolute implacability" toward "contemptible persons." And precisely in those areas where propaganda is most important, the "unfavorable terrain" of thickly settled farmland or suburbs, the guerrillas must eliminate "recalcitrant enemies . . . without leniency when they constitute a danger. . . . There can be no enemies in vital positions within the area of operation." On the other hand, he insists that terrorism "is a negative weapon which produces in no way the desired effects, which can turn a people against a given revolutionary movement, and which brings with it a loss of lives among those taking part that is much greater than the return." The rejection of terror is thus a practical, not a moral decision.

Terror, less violent forms of coercion, and even sabotage, if it destroys the livelihood of the poor, may backlash and repel rather than attract popular support. Clearly, these techniques must at times be employed by any guerrilla force, but the problems of when and how to use them, and how to keep them under control, are extremely difficult ones. Widespread use of terror worked rather well for the Greek Communist rebels in the late 1940's; nevertheless, it finally drove over a half-million of what should have been their strongest supporters into the cities and contributed to the eventual Communist defeat. Terror was effective in Cyprus against a British government without sufficient political strength or will; it failed in Malaya against a British government determined and able to resist and to wait.

The last, and perhaps the gravest, dilemma confronting the guerrilla commander is that of pushing the war to a victorious conclusion. Guevara orthodoxly states that partisans must eventually regularize their operations if they are to win. Unconventional warfare becomes conventional as guerrillas grow stronger and their opponents weaker. Since the vicious but inept Batista regime made the problem almost academic for the Cuban revolutionaries, Guevara's general assertion of the problem is backed by little specific advice on how to achieve regularization. But if the incumbent power has military strength combined with the will and the intelligence to use it, then the guerrilla leader will have to recognize that irregular warfare alone will not succeed, but is simply the means of converting popular support into an army sufficient for the climactic military encounters.

The guerrilla leader's principal difficulty will then be to time the transition to regular forces and conventional tactics. Mao warns of guerrillaism, of overlong attachment to irregular organization and methods; regularization unduly delayed exhausts the popular base of the struggle. Historically, the opposite error seems more common, as guerrillas succumb to the lure of uniforms, of heavy weapons, of being able to sleep at night, and of conventional, orderly battle. Often a diplomatic factor is also at work, since foreign governments seem to see in the existence of a regular army a tangible guarantee of the movement's eventual success. The step of regularization may then be taken to help obtain diplomatic recognition, and thus achieve an important political goal. Taken prematurely, however, it grants a strong incumbent the opportunity that guerrilla tactics deny him: to hit an enemy that cannot melt away. Both the FLN, in Algeria, and the Vietminh appear to have committed this error, although they recovered from their defeats; the Greek Communists made the mistake and did not recover.[2]

One prerequisite of regularization is the establishment of territorial base areas. As Guevara points out, even in the early stages of guerrilla war such bases offer the considerable advantage of rest, training, supply, and medical care. But a base area provides the sort of fixed target that increases the danger of a crippling blow. Rough terrain is useful but cannot in itself make a base area inaccessible to a competent modern force. Mao describes the development of "flexible bases," but these would seem to require both an area of operations and a sophistication of civilian underground organization that must be considered exceptional. Guevara discusses the value of a "secure" base; how to render it secure against a strong opponent without resorting to

[2] Colonel T. Papathanasiades, "The Bandits' Last Stand in Greece," *Military Review*, XXX (February, 1951), 24–26.

disadvantageous positional warfare he does not make clear.

External sanctuaries, such as Tunisia has provided for the FLN, are a partial alternative to internal base areas. In fact, there is little historical evidence to support the proposition that without outside help, guerrillas can win against an incumbent who is politically and militarily strong, unless, that is, the incumbent decides the game is not worth the candle. To a large extent, as Guevara notes, guerrilla warfare can and must be self-sustaining: The people provide food and shelter; the enemy furnishes small arms and ammunition. Both Guevara and the FLN leadership have emphasized the logistical and even morale advantages that accrue if guerrillas use the weapons of the enemy rather than foreign calibers, which, incidentally, suggests one reason for the surprising coolness of the Algerian rebels toward Communist aid. But some foreign assistance appears to be crucial for eventual success, and in particular for the transition to regular operations. It may happen, however, that foreign aid dampens the emotions that provide the fuel for guerrilla warfare, and renders the ideological struggle more difficult. Inevitably there will be some conflict between the aims of indigenous guerrillas and their foreign benefactors and it would be unrealistic to assume that this conflict can be permanently ignored or concealed. If there is a racial difference as well, or if the guerrilla movement itself is a nationalistic insurrection, then friction between what have been called the internal and the external fronts may be a major obstacle to success. The incumbent power will always try to exploit the facts or legends of foreign support, and thus attack the very basis of the insurgents' motives.

In all these dilemmas, the guerrilla leader must display exceptional judgment. Too much boldness can be as fatal as too much caution. The distance between the two is less than in conventional warfare, and a shrewd opponent will act so as to make it narrower still. There are many ways for the guerrilla leader to be wrong, but only one way for him to be right.

What Cyprus and Cuba were in miniature, the seven-year-long war in Algeria has been on a larger and bloodier scale. The military effort of the Algerian nationalists has consisted of guerrilla operations, backed by a small force of regulars, and of terror. Terror is employed both against the French and as a means of keeping their own adherents in line. Foreign support provides equipment, diplomatic assistance, and bases for organizing and training. The whole makes up a perfect example of what the French have come to call "revolutionary" or "subversive" warfare.

In the doctrine of *guerre révolutionnaire,* certain groups in the French army have attempted to collect and synthesize the whole range of modern unconventional warfare. Briefly, the basic characteristics of the

french doctrine

doctrine have been expressed by them in an equation: guerrilla warfare + psychological warfare = revolutionary warfare. The terms should of course be taken in their broadest sense. "Guerrilla warfare" emphasizes the importance of actions by individuals and small groups—sabotage, terror, ambushes and raids—without denigrating the use of large formations. "Psychological warfare" defines all violent and nonviolent measures undertaken *primarily* to influence the opponent rather than to annihilate him. This may mean anything from a local rumor to clandestine indoctrination of civilians and full-scale diplomatic action. The doctrine's salient point is the complete interdependence between violence and nonviolence, not alone in the methods used but also in the targets chosen. "Revolutionary warfare" postulates insurgents who will direct their efforts at least as much at the inhabitants of the territory whose control is at stake as against the armed forces of the incumbent.[3]

Against such an opponent, conventional military methods are obviously insufficient. The French theorists have grasped the operational significance of the political factor, and have attempted to integrate it into their own weapons systems, in the form of psychological warfare, re-education, indoctrination of their own cadres, and

3 See Peter Paret, "The French Army and la Guerre Révolutionnaire," *Journal of the Royal United Service Institution,* CIV (February, 1959), 59–69; reprinted in *Survival,* I (March–April, 1959), 25–32.

shaping of government policy. But they have not been able to formulate a political alternative that would appeal as strongly to the Algerians as it did to themselves, and in the process they have gone far toward disrupting the army and the nation. Their example of copying the enemy's methods too closely is one for U.S. military forces to avoid.

THE TASKS OF COUNTERGUERRILLA ACTION

What are the conditions for successful counterguerrilla action? Combating guerrillas is both a military and a political problem. Much depends on the stage of development of the guerrillas. Different tactics must be used against them depending on whether they are well established, closely identified with the population, or just beginning the process of indoctrination and organization. But in no case will military or political measures by themselves solve the problem.

Counterguerrilla action may be separated into three major tasks. Generally, these must be pursued simultaneously since success in one area depends on progress in the others. In a very real sense, it is only for purposes of analysis that they can be discussed separately. The tasks are:

1. The military defeat of the guerrilla forces.
2. The separation of the guerrilla from the population.

3. The re-establishment of governmental authority and the development of a viable social order.

It is erroneous to think that military defeat pure and simple will be a final solution. Unless the population has been weaned away from the guerrilla and his cause, unless reforms and re-education have attacked the psychological base of guerrilla action, unless the political network backing him up has been destroyed, military defeat is only a pause and fighting can easily erupt again.

The worst military mistake in fighting guerrillas is to treat them as if they were conventional opponents. In the long run, the ability to control certain pieces of ground, or to mount periodic expeditions into and out of a particular area, means little in this sort of warfare. Instead, the security of one's own base and rear is essential; the strategic offensive must be deliberately cautious and carefully coordinated, although tactical movement can be rapid, even daring. The French during much of the Indochinese war seem to have reversed these principles; strategically audacious, their tactics were marked by road-bound movements and hedgehog defense. On more than one occasion, they struck deep into the Vietminh base area without previously or even simultaneously taking elementary precautions to protect their own lines of communication and supply.

All successful counterguerrilla operations—in Greece,

South Korea, the Philippines, and Malaya—have combined mobile striking forces with close territorial control. Territorial control has always been achieved by dividing the combat zone into areas and assigning to each more or less stationary units that act as both defenders and police. The striking forces, on the other hand, are more centrally located and directed, and must have maximum mobility.

There has been some confusion over the types of forces involved in counterguerrilla action and their respective roles. The territorial units are regulars, reservists, militia, or augmented police. The mobile striking forces require the very best regulars, organized and trained to fight unorthodoxly but exploiting all their inherent advantages. It is dangerous to rely too heavily on the technological means available to modern regular troops, but the imaginative combination of these means with unconventional tactics may very well be decisive. The mobile striking forces thus cannot consist of hastily recruited and trained progovernment civilians; on the contrary, they must be tough, disciplined, and thoroughly professional.

Just how professional forces may learn and employ irregular tactics is not so easily answered, and a solution may be more difficult than most soldiers realize; certainly the roots of the problem go deeper than their own alleged conservatism when face to face with a new situation. There are crucial differences between tactical operations against a conventional opponent and those against guerrillas; against the latter, for instance, physical destruction of the enemy becomes relatively more important, control of key terrain less. Not only must doctrine, training, and organization shift when dealing with a different kind of opponent, but effective counterguerrilla tactics seem to require a different combat style, perhaps the harder to achieve because style is so much a matter of attitude and is usually taken for granted. Here it may be noted that the FLN claims that the previous regular experience of many of their fighters has often proved a disadvantage in irregular combat, while one British battalion commander in Malaya found recent conscripts better suited to certain unorthodox tasks than long-service regulars.[4] At the same time, it is most unlikely that military amateurism in itself can ever be a virtue.

In an important sense, guerrillas fight in a natural manner, their organization and tactics reflecting the popular, extralegal base from which they operate. Regular troops, on the other hand, even when employing irregular tactics, operate from a governmental, legal base, and appear to suffer from attitudinal and structural inhibitions that must first be recognized if they

4 Chanderli, interview March 2 and 3, 1961.

are to be overcome.[5] A simple diagram may clarify this point, which is too often insufficiently appreciated:

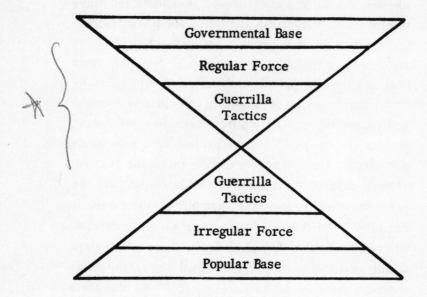

Although there may be a limited role for counter-guerrilla guerrillas, the great weakness of the mobile striking forces—imperfect tactical intelligence—is better corrected by the creation of local militia. But neither pro-government guerrillas nor militia can be effective without firm popular support.[6] And this leads to the

[5] Stanislaw Andrzejewski touches on these problems in *Military Organization and Society* (London, 1954).

[6] Examples for this abound. To cite only one instance: On one of the few occasions when French counterguerrilla guerrillas in Indochina enjoyed some success against the Vietminh forces, a Communist political commissar reported: "The reason for the great

second concern of counterguerrilla forces: Good troops employing proper tactics cannot make up for an unsound governmental and political base. The sound antipartisan tactical doctrine conceived and employed by the Germans in Russia and Yugoslavia could not compensate for a criminal political and administrative policy.

How deny the guerrilla his popular base? He must lose his hold over the people, and be isolated from them. Various techniques are available, and probably all of them would have to be used against a strong guerrilla movement.

Military defeat of the guerrilla forces, widely and persuasively publicized, is among the strongest ways of convincing people that support of the guerrillas is unwise. But such defeat is unlikely in the early stages of the conflict. A more comprehensive psychological warfare program is an obvious necessity. The program, however, must be sophisticated—as such programs have seldom been—since it must operate on the premise that the target of the program probably has more accurate information concerning the guerrillas than does the government.

To make untrue or distorted assertions to the people can be fatal. Indeed, it might be better to think of the

---

extension of the [pro-French] rebel movement and why it succeeds in holding out against us stems from the fact that we are not supported by public opinion." Quoted in Bernard Fall, *Street Without Joy* (Harrisburg, Pa., 1961), 247.

program as public information rather than psychological warfare, because its second requirement is not to confuse people who are potentially sympathetic to the guerrillas with the guerrillas themselves (who should be attacked in a separate, tailor-made program). As Lucian Pye pointed out in his study of guerrilla Communism in Malaya, the temptation to treat *all* Malayan Chinese as potential guerrillas or Communists was very great.[7] To have succumbed to it, however, would have meant establishing the very link the government had to break. Finally, public information will have little permanent effect without a long-term program of education or re-education, but this is more properly a part of the government's third task.

A standard technique in denying the guerrilla his popular base is the resettlement of populations. Resettlement has been successful with the Chinese squatters in Malaya, and partially so with the Arabs in Algeria and the Boers in South Africa. But when calculating the military advantages of resettlement and planning the details of the program, full weight must be given to its political, economic, and social effects.[8]

[7] *Guerrilla Communism in Malaya: Its Social and Political Meaning* (Princeton, N.J., 1956). See also his "Lessons from the Malayan Struggle Against Communism" and "The Policy Implications of Social Change in Non-Western Societies" (Communist Bloc Program Parts 17 and 18 [mimeographed], Center for International Studies, Massachusetts Institute of Technology [1957]).

[8] For an account of the mishandling of resettlement in South Vietnam, see Stanley Karnow, "Diem Defeats His Own Best Troops," *The Reporter*, January 19, 1961, p. 26.

Rarely can guerrillas be isolated from the people without the use of unusually harsh coercive measures. Nevertheless, counterguerrillas must comprehend that their mission is essentially conservative, while that of the guerrillas is destructive. Unless harsh measures are employed rationally and with the clear understanding by all that they are emergency measures, to be stopped as soon as possible, they may actually break down the sense of security with which the legitimacy of any non-totalitarian government is inextricably linked.

The conduct of troops and police in the field can easily undo governmental propaganda or policy, however wise in conception these may be. To cite two cases among many, police brutality—tardily stopped—in South Korea and the Philippines was of considerable benefit to the Communists.[9] The history of the Indochinese war is replete with incidents that show not French ruthlessness, but rather the failure of French leaders to make a determined effort to curb the usual roughness with which troops on active duty treat sullen, uncommunicative civilians—and, at times, innocent bystanders. A cargo plane receives antiaircraft fire; in consequence, two fighters napalm a nearby village, not knowing whether the village is pro-Communist or not. Infantrymen, after a sweltering all-day crawl in the mud, spring

[9] Lieutenant Colonel John E. Beebe, "Beating the Guerrillas in South Korea," *Military Review*, XXXV (December, 1955), 16; Major K. M. Hammer, "Huks in the Philippines," *ibid.*, XXXVI (April, 1956), 50–54; Brian Crozier, *The Rebels* (Boston, 1960), p. 217.

a trap on a suspected village but find no guerrillas; they shoot down an unarmed young man who acts suspiciously, and compensate themselves for their trouble by liberating any poultry within reach. Legionnaires decide to flatten three "sassy" villages by calling for an air strike on them.[10]

Such conduct is understandable, and to prevent it requires unusual self-restraint as well as discipline, which in turn will be possible only when commanders themselves are convinced that fair dealing with the population is as much a part of effective military action as aggressive patrolling. Correct treatment of civilians who seem to have done nothing to merit it is perhaps no more unnatural than combat itself, and it needs to be incorporated into the framework of military thought. Results in the field may not be immediately apparent, but without such behavior, there is little hope of redressing, in Guevara's words, "the notable difference that exists between the information which the rebel forces possess and the information which the enemies possess."

Even under the most extreme provocation, the same principle applies. The pressure to meet terror with counterterror will at times seem irresistible, but to do so is to play the guerrilla's game without his particular advantages. Brutality, fear, and the resultant social disorganization can work only for the guerrillas, no matter

10 Fall, *op. cit.*, pp. 105, 108, 254–55.

who initiates them. By forcing the legitimate power to adopt their own methods, the guerrillas gain a vital point. All government is based on the discriminating application of power; its indiscriminate use over extended periods implies a surrender both of policy and of ethics, and releases the kind of internal conflict that frequently destroys the capacity of a political and social organism to defend itself.

The ultimate technique in isolating guerrillas from the people is to persuade the people to defend themselves. Militia-type local defense units help in the military defeat of the guerrillas. They may gradually replace the garrison forces, freeing regulars for mobile operations. They protect their communities, ambush raiders, and furnish intelligence and security to mobile forces in the vicinity. But at least as important is their political function: Once a substantial number of members of a community commit violence on behalf of the government, they have gone far to break permanently the tie between that community and the guerrillas.

The third and final task of counterguerrilla action is the re-establishment of authority and the creation of a more stable society. The obvious first step is a program to allay the grievances that originally permitted the outbreak of violence. But, again drawing on Pye's study of Malaya, reform is not as easy as it may seem. By itself, economic aid is not enough. Reform must have at least two aspects if it is to be effective. First, the administration of reform must be reasonably honest; not only must it not be compromised by corruption, but it must not seem to be simply responding to the program of the guerrillas. Economic and social problems must be attacked on their own merits, and not as if the government were itself a political party. Ramón Magsaysay, who defeated the Huk rebellion, demonstrated that the link between guerrilla warfare and social reform was as much one of credibility as of action.

Second, and even more difficult, is the fostering of political activity, including political groups critical of government policy. Despite certain obvious disadvantages, legal political activity provides a third choice for discontented persons otherwise forced to choose between supporting the government or the guerrillas. It also keeps the government in touch with the sources of discontent.

In re-establishing their authority, can governments hope to substitute a counterideology for any ideology the guerrilla movement may have? The answer is probably no. The current assumption that the popular mind, especially in illiterate, unsophisticated societies, can be manipulated at will is false. Unlike machine-gun bolts, ideologies are not easily interchangeable. The French tried it with little success in Algeria; nationalism was too strong for them. Communism takes hold because it exploits real aspirations and convictions, not through any magic power. And the exploitation is a long-term process. Non-Communist governments should recognize that developing a counterideology is also a long-term process, and that probably the best they can hope for in fighting guerrillas is to neutralize their ideological appeal by undercutting it rather than by complete substitution.[11]

Thus the tasks of counterguerrilla warfare are as much political as military—or even more so; the two continually interact. As with the guerrillas themselves, political considerations may often have to override military considerations if permanent success is to be achieved. Tactical victories are of little value if they compromise the strategic objective. Because the true objective of guerrilla warfare is control of the people, this is one type of war in which friend-or-foe thinking is inapplicable. The greatest danger for the counterguerrilla is to succumb to the lure of a shallow opportunism: To employ the troops of a politically discredited faction or of an unpopular foreign power simply because they are available is to sacrifice ultimate prospects for immediate convenience. The hard way is often the best way.

---

11 In its efforts to present the Moslems with an acceptable political alternative to independence, the French army has generally overemphasized the role of effective techniques, while the actual content of the proposals has seemed of secondary importance. See Peter Paret, "A Total Weapon of Limited War," *Journal of the Royal United Service Institution*, CV (February, 1960), 67.

V

Guerrillas and
American Policy

These are general considerations which would seem to
apply to guerrillas anywhere. But what about the United
States? Today, guerrilla warfare concerns the United
States in three different realms of military policy:

1. In raising American and allied guerrilla potential to strengthen our ability to resist conventional
   or nuclear attack.
2. In bolstering the defenses of a friendly nation or
   government threatened by guerrillas or actually
   fighting them.
3. In employing guerrillas as offensive weapons.

Too often these problems are confused, or lumped
together under vague demands that we must expand our
unconventional warfare capabilities. But they involve
different considerations, and should be kept distinct
from one another.

DEFENSIVE USE OF GUERRILLAS

Discussion of the first problem—using guerrillas defensively—must of necessity be highly speculative. The resistance movements during World War II were *ad hoc* responses, and tell us little about the feasibility and the specific difficulties of forming such forces before the outbreak of hostilities. Some work, certainly, can be done in organizing and training to prepare people to carry on resistance that will render them more indigestible for a conventionally armed invader, or to help them conduct the broken-back war that may follow thermonuclear strikes. Among the difficulties here is the fact that the type of organization to be created depends for its effectiveness almost wholly on the maintenance of security. In peacetime, however, the security of an afterhours military organization cannot be guaranteed. Its personnel will be known, it will be open to infiltration, stocks of arms and equipment can scarcely remain hidden. It is also possible that many who picture themselves as guerrillas now may not in fact possess the needed qualities. The natural selectivity of guerrilla recruitment in wartime usually makes it difficult for an enemy to lay hands on a talkative fighter; prewar recruitment, on the contrary, might well enable him to gain the information about personnel, arms caches, and unit deployment that could result in an early defeat of the resistance movement. An attempt to stockpile the components of guerrilla warfare may thus prove worse than useless.

This is not to say that such difficulties necessarily preclude the organizing of guerrilla forces in peacetime. For example, over the past decade the East German regime has raised a sizable body of partisan groups— the so-called *Kampfgruppen*—which owe their inception to Communist leader Walter Ulbricht's call, in July, 1952, for the militarization of the East German people.[1] Officially, the partisans now number above 300,000 men, of whom somewhat more than half regularly drill and take part in training exercises. They are volunteers who have sworn to obey the orders of the Communist Party and are either Communists themselves or are considered politically reliable by the Party. They are grouped according to occupation in undersized companies; most are industrial workers, but units are also made up of such professions as teachers and civil servants. Each group is commanded by a police officer, who supervises training and is assisted by a three-man staff responsible for organization, finance and equipment, and political instruction. Ultimate control, however, rests not with the military commander but with the local Party Secretary, who alone can order mobilization and the issue of weapons, which are stored in police armories. Several *Kampfgruppen* may form a battalion. Since January,

[1] See Gerhard Baumann, "Der militärische Wert der SED-Kampfgruppen," *Wehrkunde*, VIII (October, 1959), 520–27.

1959, their organization, administration, and military training have been controlled by an office in the Ministry of National Defense, while the Central Committee of the Communist Party is responsible for their ideological indoctrination.

The members of the *Kampfgruppen* wear uniforms and carry carbines and pistols. Some units are also equipped with machine guns, and a few have armored cars and light antitank guns. Their military and political training, for which they receive no pay, takes place after hours and on weekends. The military part consists in marksmanship, care of equipment, open-order drill, small-unit tactics, cross-country marches, antisabotage action, the defense of factories and offices, and street fighting. Larger exercises are undertaken in cooperation with the army, the police, and other paramilitary organizations. As a special armed force at the disposal of the Communist Party, the *Kampfgruppen* are designed to help in the military and political indoctrination of their countrymen, to help ensure internal security, and to act as a home-defense force in times of war or of civil war.[2] How reliable and effective they would be in a crisis cannot be foretold. Occasional articles in the East German press on reluctance of members to give up free time for training suggest that even authoritarian regimes may find it a problem to forge

---

2 Baumann writes that the *Kampfgruppen* also have an aggressive role, but offers no concrete evidence for this (*ibid.*, p. 522).

a useful home-defense guerrilla force in peacetime.

Where would such forces be useful to the United States? Western Europe and the so-called gray areas—the southern rim of Asia, Latin America, the Middle East, and Africa—are the obvious possibilities. Recent unofficial proposals for the reorganization and expansion of NATO units along territorial lines imply that these formations would be expected to fight for extended periods in the enemy rear, since it would be unrealistic to expect territorial units, more lightly armed than regular divisions and composed largely of reservists or short-term conscripts, to conduct either positional or mobile defense against heavy armored attack. One proponent of territorial reorganization, admitting the guerrilla implications of his plan, has argued that Western Europe needs to acquire the "Spanish complex"; unable to exclude the invader, it should let him in and then chop him to death. Beneath the argument lurks the suggestion that Western European society does not at present have the collective fortitude for this kind of defense.

The question of Western courage and determination can hardly be discussed here. But morale is far from the only factor to be considered in any scheme to supplement or even replace NATO conventional divisions with units designed to fight as guerrillas. In the second half of the twentieth century, Europe, excepting perhaps the Balkans and the Iberian peninsula, no longer affords very favorable ground for guerrillas. Its high density of population and of communications and its comparatively accessible terrain—barring a few natural redoubts such as the Alps—seem to make rural-based guerrilla operations on a large scale highly improbable. The prospects for effective resistance through massive urban terrorism and sabotage are no more promising. A powerful occupying force, determined to impose its control and deterred by neither scruples nor military threats from the outside, can subjugate any city, as General Massu and his paratroopers convincingly demonstrated in Algiers.

Some commentators, to be sure, have reached the opposite conclusion, and their case should not go unmentioned. General Nemo, one of the theorists of *guerre révolutionnaire,* has argued that "in Europe the complex of social life renders the different elements dependent on one another. The administrative machine and the economic organization are cogs in a complex system which it is relatively easy to block. The higher the degree to which a country has evolved, and the more complex its structure, the more opportunities it offers for subversive action. . . . The European countries are fragile."[3] He concludes that guerrilla warfare in Europe is most feasible after nuclear attacks.

3 General J. M. Nemo, "The Place of Guerrilla Action in War," *Military Review,* XXXVII (November, 1957), 104–5. See also Lieutenant General D. Kveder, "Territorial War: The New Concept of Resistance," *ibid.,* XXXIV (July, 1954), 46–58.

57

General Nemo is undoubtedly right in believing that an industrialized society is sensitive to violent attack. But a foreign military government, with a coercive apparatus largely independent of the society which it has taken over, is not nearly so sensitive. Moreover, General Nemo neglects the problem of physical survival that would confront an active resistance movement operating in a constricted, densely populated area. In short, the conditions he describes are not those favorable for guerrilla warfare but for a *coup d'état*—hardly an effective weapon against a foreign invader.

Geographically and demographically, the gray areas are obviously well suited for guerrilla warfare. In these areas, the principal obstacle is probably psychological. The defensive employment of guerrillas means that it is the state, as embodied in the current regime, that is being defended. The consequent necessity of acquiring essential popular support by appealing to national sentiment raises two questions: Can nationalism in a given state be exploited, especially in the rural areas, as a fighting faith? If the answer to the first question is affirmative, can the existing government successfully identify itself with that nationalism?

Originating so largely in dislike and fear of the West, gray-area nationalism may prove difficult to shift against a new and different threat to the postcolonial state. Only if the government can make itself the focus rather than the target of nationalism, and if the urban intellectuals, who generally hold this feeling most eloquently, can and will transmit it to the peasantry, will the basic political requirements for defensive guerrilla warfare be fulfilled.

Although invasion in its classic form no longer seems to be an urgent problem in the gray areas, it is probably worthwhile to create guerrilla-type forces wherever these political requirements can be met. With careful attention to the differences between resisting external, regular attack and resisting internal, guerrilla attack, it may be possible to organize dual-purpose units that can act either as guerrillas or as counterguerrillas. But the distinction between trying to overthrow a regime and trying to defend one must have military implications—especially for recruitment, equipment, tactical doctrine, and deployment—and ought not to be ignored. The prewar organization of guerrillas, highly motivated and closely tied to localities as they are, may also have the bonus effect of providing a countersubversive force, a pressing need in the gray areas.

DEFENSE AGAINST GUERRILLAS

Quite different from using guerrillas defensively is the matter of assisting a friendly nation against them. Obviously, the United States can help equip and train counterguerrilla forces overseas. The gains derived from such a policy may be considerable, but it is well to remember that difficulties are also involved. There is, for one, the matter of relations between U.S. instructors and foreign personnel. The question "Who is boss?" will always be an irritant, and more so in the midst of politico-military conflict than in old-fashioned conventional operations. In these circumstances, self-denial, tact, and the ability to accept other peoples' ways and attitudes are essential for U.S. instructors. Emphatically, they should not be missionaries of American plenty and ease, of the material aspects of the American Way of Life.

It is also obvious that military aid offers an easy target for propaganda. The presence of American advisers and instructors can be exploited to throw doubt on the patriotism and independence of the regime they are trying to help. The military advantages gained from improved operational efficiency must be weighed against possible psychological setbacks, which translate themselves so readily into military consequences in guerrilla warfare.

These are relatively minor points. Of real importance is the problem of achieving a suitable political base from which to combat guerrillas. Today, most areas throughout the world that are actually threatened by irregular warfare stand in need of profound social, economic, and political reforms. The regimes in many of these areas may be unwilling, or consider themselves unable, to meet the need. How far is the United States ready to compel them to make the necessary changes?

A regime's willingness to institute reforms is, however, only one side of the question. What kinds of reform are acceptable to the United States, and what kinds would it consider intolerable? It is in the economic field that this problem becomes especially troublesome. Although industrialization and land reform offer American industry new opportunities, former investments and special privileges are often lost in the process. Pressures on the government not to support programs that involve expropriation of American property will always be powerful. Leaving private interests aside, to what extent is the United States willing to let capitalism be blended with socialism in the gray areas of the world?[4] It is clear that, in spite of our desire to remove poverty and injustice of all kinds from the earth, we find it more difficult than the Communists do to back radical reform movements. But it is exactly these movements that, in danger zones like Central and South America and Southeast Asia, tend to attract wide popular support.

There has been some reaction within the United States to the assumption that guerrilla warfare and social dislocation are closely interrelated. It has

[4] On this point, see the excellent, succinct discussion "The Limits of Cubanism," *The Economist*, April 22, 1961, 338–39.

been argued that the idea "that guerrilla warfare cannot be won unless peoples are dissatisfied" is, at best, half true, and that Communist guerrillas are gaining "for very simple reasons known as guns, bombs, fighters, and threats."[5] If these arguments mean that reform cannot be a substitute for an effective military response, then they are correct. But if they mean that reform is irrelevant or nonessential, they ignore the following obvious facts: (1) Communist guerrillas have acquired popular support in these areas and have kept it from their enemies; (2) such popular support is not obtained simply by terror and propaganda, however useful these techniques may be, but by combining genuine aspirations and grievances with an absolute confidence in ultimate victory; and (3) military defeat of guerrillas is extremely difficult, if not impossible, to achieve until they lose the supplies, intelligence, and security that popular support provides.

[5] The first statement is that of Walt W. Rostow, then the President's Special Assistant for National Security Affairs, addressing the Army Special Warfare School at Fort Bragg, N.C.; the second is that of Eric Sevareid paraphrasing Secretary of Defense McNamara. Mr. Sevareid's syndicated column was reprinted in full in *The Reporter*, July 6, 1961, p. 13, and quoted extensively in *Life*, June 30, 1961, p. 42. Mr. Rostow's speech was reported more fully in the *Washington Post*, June 29, 1961, p. C-16, than elsewhere, but the passages quoted here and below are taken from the full text. In fairness to Mr. Rostow's analysis of guerrilla warfare, an earlier remark in his speech should also be cited: "To understand this problem . . . one must begin with the great revolutionary process that is going forward in the southern half of the world; for the guerrilla warfare problem in these areas is a product of that revolutionary process and the Communist effort and intent to exploit it."

OFFENSIVE USE OF GUERRILLAS

These problems must be faced whenever the question is that of bolstering another country's defenses against internal aggression. They would redouble in force whenever the United States should choose to employ guerrillas offensively. But a decision of this sort would involve the United States in an additional range of problems of far greater magnitude. Advocates of the offensive employment of guerrillas have given these problems too little consideration; rather, they have stressed the supposed advantages of offensive employment—that it would be economical in money and manpower, that it would present fewer risks than nuclear or conventional strategies, and that it would enable the United States to seize the initiative in the Cold War.[6] Closer attention to the questions of where and why this strategy might be employed promises a more balanced view.

There are three sets of circumstances under which the United States may want to use guerrillas as an offensive weapon: to deter or to fight a general war; to apply direct pressure against the Soviet Union or Red China for some more limited strategic purpose; and to make

6 For a scholarly example of this point of view, see Slavko N. Bjelajac, "Unconventional Warfare in the Nuclear Era," *Orbis,* IV (Fall, 1960), 323–37; for a popular one, see "The American Guerrillas: How to Multiply Small Numbers by an Anti-Communist Factor," *Time,* March 10, 1961, p. 19.

local, or tactical, changes along the Cold War perimeter.

Certainly, it is feasible for the United States to prepare now to start guerrilla warfare behind the Iron Curtain in case of a massive nuclear or conventional Communist attack.[7] Especially in the NATO area, where our limited-war forces are still so obviously inadequate, Western capability for this kind of guerrilla response to large-scale aggression will strengthen our deterrent posture by adding to the costs that the Soviet Union must reckon on. Terrain becomes generally more favorable for guerrilla warfare east of the Elbe, while the uprisings in East Germany, Hungary, and Poland indicate that discontent may be strong enough to support it, especially with Communist troops busy elsewhere. The provocativeness of stationing near the Iron Curtain the special units that would trigger such action is a minor consideration. A major problem would be organizing an underground net in the satellites, which would render these units far more effective than if they had to rely on improvised contacts.

The use of guerrillas as a strategic weapon in a more limited clash involves greater difficulties. Whether they are being employed during a specific crisis, like that over Berlin, or in a more general attempt to apply continuous counterpressure on the Communist bloc, the guerrillas themselves and their civilian supporters will be

[7] See Robert W. van de Velde, "The Neglected Deterrent," *Military Review*, XXXVIII (August, 1958), 3–10.

engaged in what for them is most likely a forlorn hope.[8] Effective pressure points are necessarily places of vital concern to the Russians or Chinese; their own home-lands, the East European satellites, North Korea, and Tibet readily come to mind. The very significance of the area attacked would ensure severe repressive meas-ures rather than a softening of the regime. Established Communist governments are past masters of this kind of warfare and could be expected to react ruthlessly and efficiently. It is doubtful whether the guerrillas could ever win locally without overt armed support from the United States, and this would seem out of the question. In other words, the United States would be asking these people to act as expendable pawns in our global strategy. Not only might we be reluctant to do this, but they might understandably refuse, since loss of confidence in ultimate victory inevitably means loss of popular sup-port and collapse of guerrilla morale.

Is there a serious danger of escalation to greater vio-lence in the strategic employment of guerrillas in lim-ited conflict? Of all forms of warfare, irregular opera-tions are most difficult to calculate and to control. Their employment in areas vital to the opponent ensures that his response will be strong. Once involved, the United

8 For the first possibility, see Morton A. Kaplan, *The Strategy of Lim-ited Retaliation* (Policy Memorandum No. 19, Center of International Studies, Princeton University [1959]); for the second, see Robert Strausz-Hupé, William R. Kintner, and Stefan T. Possony, *A Forward Strategy for America* (New York, 1961); especially pp. 29–31, 38, 158–60.

States might easily find that its prior estimates of the situation were mistaken, and that it was facing an unpleasant choice between abandoning friends or raising the stakes to an unintended level. On the other hand, if the guerrilla offensive should prove unexpectedly successful, say in Eastern Europe, the Soviet Union might well consider direct surprise attack to eliminate the instigator of rebellion rather than accept the disruption of her satellite buffer.[9]

Finally, the United States may want to use guerrillas tactically, to overthrow a government, Communist or non-Communist, that is sufficiently obnoxious to us. The weakest Communist states on the periphery, like North Vietnam, are possible candidates, as are those which seem to be near-satellites, like Cuba. A few years ago, some would have added Egypt or Iraq to the list, which demonstrates the danger of being too quick on the guerrilla trigger. In any case, the objective would be not simply to make trouble for our enemies but to substitute a friendly, stable government for an unfriendly one. This objective, when pursued by means of guerrilla war, raises at least two questions: Can the United States reasonably expect a society profoundly damaged by internal war to be stable, without reliance on authoritarian techniques? Is the United States interested in

9 See Herman Kahn, *On Thermonuclear War* (Princeton, N.J., 1960), pp. 134–37.

such an outcome, and is it willing to bear the responsibility for liberating people by these means?

In addition to the local consequences, the international repercussions should be considered if the United States decides to use irregular warfare as a means of subversion. These repercussions go far beyond the borders of guerrilla warfare itself; they pertain to the whole question of international intervention. Guerrillas do, however, raise special problems in this area. Legally, there is an obvious if unclear distinction between espionage and violent subversion, and to engage very actively in the latter may deprive us of a large part of the cover of international law. In practice, there is a major difference between a *coup d'état* and guerrilla warfare as methods of subversion. A *coup,* such as the United States may have promoted in Guatemala and Iran, can be offered to the world as an accomplished fact, while guerrillas are unconscionably slow in their work, almost certainly entailing prolonged embarrassment for their American backers along the way. We would attempt to justify our action by invoking the higher law of human freedom. But we might be more convincing, and our embarrassment might be less, if we had a record of supporting guerrilla subversion of right-wing tyranny as well as that of the left.

It has been truly said that the Cold War is not an international popularity contest. At the same time, it would be unrealistic to ignore the possible effects on non-Communist governments if the United States adds subversive warfare to its offensive armory. If the United States uses guerrillas to overthrow unfriendly governments, we will obviously become more vulnerable than ever to the charge of "imperialism." Might this not have tangible military consequences? It may create new strains within NATO, the strength of which, after all, is our first strategic concern. It may also hamper the effectiveness of our counterguerrilla operations, by making friendly and neutralist governments under guerrilla attack in the gray areas less able to accept our help without discrediting themselves in the eyes of their own populations.

The most fundamental considerations in the use of guerrillas for subversion may indeed pertain to the United States itself. Can an open society successfully use this weapon? Not only must we act clandestinely, we must also convince bystanders, friends, even ourselves that we are not acting at all. The case of Cuba argues that our capacity for this kind of prolonged secrecy is not yet very great. As a matter of general policy, the subversive employment of guerrillas would seem to predicate an employer whose foreign policy easily incorporates the principle of aggression, who is willing and able to use totalitarian means of conflict and control, and whose ends conform to his system and his methods.

Might use of subversive weapons, including guerrillas,

damage the United States internally more than it could possibly strengthen it abroad? Undoubtedly this would depend on the extensiveness of their use, as well as on the flexibility of our current democratic condition. The effects, about which we can only speculate, might include the alienation of a numerous and influential body of citizens, who would refuse to accept the divorce of Cold War strategy from the self-restraint of law, and the encouragement of extremist groups on the right wing, who already seem to reject what may be loosely called the American consensus on values and purposes.

As a way out of these possible dilemmas, it has been suggested that the United States support but not instigate guerrilla movements aimed at unfriendly governments. The distinction is appealing and probably useful, but might be difficult to maintain in practice. Certainly its explicit enunciation as policy would tend to blur the distinction. Our recent venture in Cuba, however, indicates its practical virtue: More emphasis on support, and less on instigation, would have clarified the possibilities and the requirements for success.

CONCLUSION

In general, the aggressive employment of guerrillas except in case of international war seems of dubious value. Militarily, it is a more difficult and dangerous undertaking than is apparent from public discussion. Moreover, its political risks, both international and domestic, will in most cases outweigh the expected gains. Success and failure in guerrilla warfare carry with them peculiar moral overtones. Even though it may be the result of manipulation, the popular support guerrillas must have in order to win seems to provide a referendum affirming the rightness, if not the strict legality, of the event. Failure, on the other hand, implies that the employer of guerrilla warfare could not engage the popular interest. The United States will want to avoid this stigma, this extra penalty for defeat in guerrilla war. The practical lessons are that the subversive employment of guerrillas is not so limited a risk as it may seem, and that in order to ensure its success, the United States must make careful and elaborate estimates and preparations before launching any such venture.

It is worth noting that in the first authoritative and comprehensive statement on guerrilla warfare to come from the Kennedy Administration, Walt W. Rostow did not even mention the training or employment of guerrillas for subversive purposes by the United States. In fact, by implication, he appears to have rejected it: "Despite all the Communist talk of aiding movements of national independence, they are driven in the end, by the nature of their system, to violate the independence of nations. Despite all the Communist talk of American imperialism, we are committed, by the nature of our system, to support the cause of national independence. And the truth will come out."[10]

Unfortunately, public and Congressional concern over the employment of guerrillas by the United States has at times confused, at times overridden, the principal problem—how to fight against guerrillas. Small special units, designed to organize large groups of friendly native guerrillas, seem not wholly relevant to the most pressing guerrilla threats faced by the West. To be sure, these highly trained units are able to act as advisory groups, organizing foreign counterguerrillas. But there is little indication in the history of unconventional warfare that guerrillas themselves are effective *counterguerrilla* weapons. Only in the rare case of a country made up of several distinct and powerful ethnic groups—Algeria, for instance, or Malaya—does it seem possible for two opposed guerrilla forces each to establish the popular base essential for survival and effectiveness. Even in such circumstances, the incumbent government should seriously ponder the desirability of a strategy that would inevitably deepen an already existing split in the social and political fabric. Despite their shortcomings, conventional forces, operating from a legal base and trained for unconventional warfare, still seem to provide the best military answer to the guerrilla problem. These forces will not be a cheap solution because at least ten counterguerrillas are needed for every

[10] Address at Fort Bragg, June 28, 1961 (see n. 5).

guerrilla in the field. Unfortunately, there do not seem to be any short cuts, and even having enough of the right kinds of troops will not be sufficient in itself.

Admittedly, any rejection of the usefulness of counterguerrilla guerrillas must be a tentative judgment, based on sparse and somewhat conflicting evidence. The effectiveness of such forces belongs among the open questions of unconventional warfare, questions that require more experience and research before they can be answered with confidence. It may be useful to conclude the present study by summarizing a few of the most significant and puzzling of these problems: (1) counterguerrilla guerrillas; (2) guerrillas in urban areas; (3) terror; (4) the guerrillas' role in politicizing the population; (5) reforms; (6) the organizational difficulties faced by the United States in fighting unconventional war. All these topics have been touched on in the course of the preceding discussion; they should now be considered on their own.

(1) The idea of setting guerrilla against guerrilla is an advance over the traditional attitude, which holds that guerrillas can be defeated by conventional techniques. It indicates a more profound understanding of what guerrilla warfare is about, and has the seductive quality of fighting fire with fire. However, when one considers the concrete techniques involved, it becomes apparent that the symmetrical situation implied in the phrase cannot easily be achieved.

What are the essentials of guerrilla operations? At a minimum, guerrillas must have the ability to exist and to fight without being directly tied to a fixed administrative base. To some extent government forces can fake this mobility and independence; for example, by hiding stores of food and equipment in the countryside, they enable their units to operate away from a base for extended periods. Their tactics can also reflect those of the insurgents, and military objectives may be considered as roughly similar. Although guerrillas can derive intelligence from the population, counterguerrillas can draw on this source only to a limited extent; mostly they must depend on such methods as air observation and informers.

What can be duplicated only with difficulty is (a) the insurgents' clandestine yet close integration with the people; and (b) the guerrillas' conviction that they have no choice—they *must* live and fight as they do. One may reasonably doubt whether government forces can ever acquire the underground mentality—a mixture of fanaticism and an unrelieved sense of insecurity. Instead, it seems likely that they will be weakened by the knowledge that policy rather than need dictates their employment as guerrillas, and that they will find it difficult to gain adequate protection from the civilian population. Only if the government has the opportunity and the boldness to recruit unusual personnel—former insurgents, for example—and permits them to fight in an unorthodox political framework, does there seem any prospect for military success.

The most instructive recent example of counterguerrilla guerrillas is provided by several French-inspired operations in Algeria. Nearly all shared the same basis: a dissident Algerian leadership, whose political aims the French promised to support. It proved to be a difficult technique. The earliest counterguerrilla guerrilla unit, called "Force K" after its leader, Kobus, was raised near Algiers in 1956; its actions soon brought it into conflict with the regular forces in the area. Tighter liaison and control were introduced; a company of paratroopers was assigned as operational support; uniforms, heavy weapons, and vehicles were supplied; and the band became more and more regularized. At the same time, it was being infiltrated by the FLN. By April, 1958, the conflict of ideologies proved too great, and after massacring some pro-French members, most of Force K joined the rebels.[11]

The tendency toward playing off one side against the other appeared to be almost universal among the counterguerrilla guerrillas in Algeria, and they were of little use in the field even when the French army kept them under tight operational and administrative control. Indeed, throughout the entire seven years of the war, only

11. For a fuller discussion of French counterguerrilla guerrillas in Algeria, see Michel Déon, *L'Armée d'Algerie et la pacification* (Paris, 1959), pp. 88–119.

one guerrilla force, commanded by the former French NCO Si Cherif, enjoyed a measure of success. Social, political, and psychological factors seem to speak against the counterguerrilla guerrilla; although in circumstances different from those in Algeria he might be more successful, his case has not yet been proved.

(2) Contemporary military thought associates guerrillas with the countryside. This connection is dictated by history, most current experience, and logic. The difficulties guerrillas may experience in a densely populated area are obvious. The great number of potential informers, together with police surveillance, identity and ration cards, block wardens, security checks at work and in the streets—the whole paraphernalia of controls that can be mobilized in the modern city—handicap the movement of armed groups. The opposition is fragmented, and may find it easier to turn to conspiracy—mobilization on the political plane—or to individual action—propaganda, sabotage, assassination.

However, as was suggested on page 57, neutralizing the guerrilla potential of a city is predicated on an efficient government or occupying force, which will not hesitate to apply ruthless methods and which, moreover, is immune to subversion. An example might be a Russian army stationed in Western Europe. But military analysis cannot always presuppose high levels of efficiency and determination. Would West German urban centers be out of the question for guerrilla resistance operations if the invaders were not Russians but East Germans? Could one not imagine eventualities when cities in Latin America and Southeast Asia would constitute feasible terrain for irregulars? What seems to be decisive is whether or not the opposing army or police forces can be subverted or infiltrated. Recent events in Algeria, where the intensity and continuity of OAS operations went far beyond the bounds of what is normally considered terror, indicate the range of possibilities.

Besides, what do the labels "urban" and "rural" actually mean? Obviously, irregulars should not hole up in a single city, isolated from the countryside and from other population centers. But might they not fare better in an industrial area—the Ruhr, for example—with a close pattern of cities, towns, and open country?

(3) Terror, which guerrillas may or may not employ as a primary weapon, has received less systematic analysis than any other component of irregular war. It is a method that most of us find difficult to consider with detachment; but revulsion, although understandable, must not be permitted to interfere with our comprehension of an increasingly important phenomenon. It is essential that study be given to aspects that are of great concern to both governments and insurgents—the effectiveness of terror under different conditions, control difficulties, and the possible consequences to a cause or even to a society of its use. Here only two general observations can be made.

(a) Is it rational to single out terror for special moral censure? It is not easy to see why tossing a hand grenade into a crowded bus should be more cowardly, wanton, and sneaky than bombing a town from an airplane. In both cases, noncombatants are liable to get hurt, and, indeed, it may be among the purposes of the act to destroy civilian morale and lessen confidence in the authorities' power to protect the population. It is equally difficult to understand why it should be more honorable or take more courage to pilot a bomber than to lie in wait in a ditch. Moral judgments such as these also carry with them strong political implications. Often terror is the only method available to insurgents, so that its condemnation seems simply a declaration for the *status quo*.

(b) As prevalent as the moralizing attitude toward terror is the tendency to lump all kinds of terrorism together. In fact, there are various forms of terrorist activity and it is essential that one be able to differentiate among them. All guerrilla movements will employ a limited form of terror to discourage "treason." Then there is a selective terror to intimidate certain groups, such as government officials or a social class, and the criteria of selection may vary widely. Another type of selective terror is used to impress groups other than those under attack. Finally, terror in its "purest" form is indiscriminate, aimed at breaking down all trust, authority, and security; even here, its intensity is an important variable. Reports available to the public almost never make such distinctions.

(4) Terror as a technique for influencing behavior is clearly related to a broader question: the use of guerrilla warfare, not simply as the military means to a political end, but as a political process in itself. Mao implies that the most important aspect of guerrilla warfare may be not its effect on the enemy but its effect on the guerrilla and his supporters. The necessarily widespread and protracted experience of guerrilla warfare breaks down passivity, and trains political cadres for the postwar task of government. An atmosphere of violence creates new emotions and commitments, so that in the end a whole society may become revolutionary. The ancient concept of war revitalizing society is here given new form.

The cases where guerrilla warfare has done the opposite, producing schism and war-weariness, are numerous and unambiguous. Mao himself may have stressed the point primarily to make a political virtue out of a military necessity. At the same time, there is a certain plausibility to the idea. Violent experience does change people, whether they are perpetrators, victims, or witnesses. It might be that a culture whose way of life is traditionally hostile to violent action is more susceptible to this particular phenomenon, if and when it occurs, than is a culture that has learned to take for granted certain forms of violence, as do Western societies. The possibility of this politicizing effect of guerrilla warfare bears watching.

(5) The recurrent argument over the relevance of economic and political reform to guerrilla warfare has already been discussed. While we have no doubt that reform is relevant, it is certain that the exact nature of reform demands the most careful thought. Comprehensive change—call it modernization or Westernization—is a process that currently makes much of the world vulnerable to internal warfare; to speed and control this process is in the American interest. At the same time, it is recognized that guerrilla warfare may be initiated despite or even because of attempts to direct change.

Specific reforms, however, can drain the sources of strength of an insurgent movement. If the government correctly analyzes the social groups and psychological appeals used to recruit guerrilla leaders, fighters, and supporters, respectively, it ought to be able to make political adjustments and allocate nonmilitary resources in a militarily remunerative way. Such actions should reinforce and not obstruct the longer-term task of stabilization, but the latter must not be confused with the former.

(6) These are questions that apply to guerrilla warfare generally. There is a final question, still of general applicability, but of special importance and difficulty for the United States. How can this nation effectively manage its unconventional-warfare operations? Simply to list the interested agencies is to appreciate the magnitude of the problem: the Army, including Special Forces,

Psychological Warfare, and Civil Affairs; military assistance and advisory groups; the Central Intelligence Agency; the U.S. Information Agency; the Agency for International Development; the State Department; and generally the Marine Corps, Navy, and Air Force, as well. To coordinate political and military policy-making in the National Security Council has not been easy; can the United States harmonize action in the field, at the level of execution?

The panacea of "unification" is no answer. Not only would it be unfeasible, but it could well be dangerous, since the continuous conflict between political and military requirements in unconventional warfare should be reflected rather than masked in the organization. On the other hand, the maintenance of liaison among the various agencies is not the answer either. Something more positive is needed. To begin with, there must be a meeting of minds on the nature of the task and the general approach to it; that is, there must be the doctrinal consensus mentioned in the Introduction. Further, the officer in the field must represent his own particular interest in the struggle without viewing that interest as a holy preserve consecrated by expertise. In particular, this means that State Department officials must know enough about military problems and techniques to reject, accept, or demand modification of military plans on some intelligent and informed basis. It means that military officers must be ready to accept such "interference" as normal. If political officials instead fall back on the dogma of civilian supremacy over the military in order to keep control, then it is doubtful if the primacy of political considerations will actually be maintained in the conduct of operations. Doctrinal unity, and joint education and training, seem to promise more within the American institutional setting than does any drastic reorganization. Even the organization of unconventional-warfare divisions within the nonmilitary agencies raises the danger of creating special interests that might not truly represent the political point of view.

A successful response to the problem posed by the guerrilla is neither simple to plan nor easy, cheap, and quick to carry out. Guerrilla operations are as difficult to fight as the Cold War itself. But the first step in responding successfully is to come to terms with the reality of the world today, and this means avoiding oversimplification. Basically, the problem is political; to attempt to understand it as a purely military one is the most dangerous kind of oversimplification. Guerrillas are a symptom rather than a cause. Lasting success requires a viable political settlement, and even operational success over a period of time demands the proper political framework for effective military action.

A Selected Bibliography

I. GENERAL WORKS

ANDRZEJEWSKI, STANISLAW. *Military Organization and Society*. London, 1954.

BONNET, GABRIEL. *Les Guerres insurrectionnelles et révolutionnaires*. Paris, 1958.

CALLWELL, C. *Small Wars*. London, 1909.

CLAUSEWITZ, CARL VON. *On War*. Translated by O. S. MATTHIJS JOLLES. Washington, D.C., 1950.
The edition of *Vom Kriege* edited by Werner Hahlweg, which was published in Bonn in 1952, is the first since the original 1832 edition to contain the complete, unaltered text.

DEMANGE, COLONEL. "La guérilla," *Revue Militaire Générale*, February, May, 1960.

LENIN, VLADIMIR I. *Clausewitz' Werk vom Kriege: Auszüge und Randglossen*. East Berlin, 1957.

LIDDELL HART, BASIL H. *Strategy: The Indirect Approach*. New York, 1954.

Military Affairs, XXIV, No. 3, Fall, 1960.
Issue devoted to irregular warfare.

MODELSKI, GEORGE. *The International Relations of Internal War*. Research Monograph No. 11, Center of International Studies, Princeton University, 1961.

II. THE HISTORICAL BACKGROUND TO 1900

CAULAINCOURT, A. A. L. DE. *With Napoleon in Russia.* New York, 1935.

CUNEO, J. *Robert Rogers of the Rangers.* New York, 1959.

CUNHA, EUCLIDES DA. *Rebellion in the Backlands.* Translated by SAMUEL PUTNAM. Chicago, 1944.
The Brazilian insurrection of 1897.

ENGELS, FREDERICK. "Introduction," *The Class Struggles in France, 1848–50,* in KARL MARX, *Selected Works,* II. New York [1933?].

GNEISENAU, A. NEITHARDT VON. "Plan zur Vorbereitung eines Volksaufstandes," in G. H. PERTZ, *Das Leben des Feldmarschalls Grafen Neithardt von Gneisenau,* II. Berlin, 1865.
The most important of the plans for popular insurrection drawn up in Prussia between 1807 and 1812.

GODECHOT, JACQUES. *La Contre-révolution: 1789–1804.* Paris, 1961.

GOTTMANN, JEAN. "Bugeaud, Galliéni, Lyautey: The Development of French Colonial Warfare," in *Makers of Modern Strategy,* ed. EDWARD M. EARLE. Princeton, 1960.

GRANT, CARL E. "Partisan Warfare 1861–65," *Military Review,* XXXVIII (November, 1958).

HIGGINBOTHAM, DON. *Daniel Morgan, Revolutionary Rifleman.* Chapel Hill, N.C., 1961.

HIRN, JOSEF. *Tirols Erhebung im Jahre 1809.* Innsbruck, 1909.
An account of the popular uprising in the Tyrol in 1809.

HOWARD, MICHAEL. *The Franco-Prussian War.* London, 1961.

JONES, VIRGIL C. *Ranger Mosby.* Durham, N.C., 1944.

KRUGER, RAYNE. *Good-bye Dolly Gray: The Story of the Boer War.* Philadelphia, 1960.

McCRADY, EDWARD. *History of South Carolina in the Revolution.* 2 vols. New York, 1901–2.

MURRAY, KEITH A. *The Modocs and Their War.* Norman, Okla., 1959.
Nineteenth-century Indian warfare in the U.S.

NEUMANN, SIGMUND. "Engels and Marx: Military Concepts of the Social Revolutionaries," in *Makers of Modern Strategy,* ed. EDWARD M. EARLE. Princeton, 1960.

OMAN, SIR CHARLES. *A History of the Peninsular War.* 8 vols. London, 1902–30.

PARET, PETER. *Internal War and Pacification: The Vendée, 1789–1796.* Research Monograph No. 12, Center of International Studies, Princeton University, 1961.

PECKHAM, HOWARD H. *Pontiac and the Indian Uprising.* Princeton, 1949.

REITZ, DENEYS. *Commando.* New York, 1930.
The Boer War.

ROCCA, A. J. M. *Memoirs of the War of the French in Spain.* London, 1815.
One of the best eyewitness accounts of Spanish guerrilla warfare against the French.

RÖSSLER, HELLMUTH. *Österreichs Kampf um Deutschlands Befreiung,* I. Hamburg, 1940.
A history of Austrian opposition to Napoleon, with material on various attempts to organize insurrections against the French.

TEBBEL, JOHN, and JENNISON, KEITH. *The American Indian Wars.* New York, 1960.

TROW, HARRISON. *Charles W. Quantrell.* Kansas City, Mo., 1923.

WOLFF, LEON. *Little Brown Brother: How the United States Purchased and Pacified the Philippine Islands at the Century's Turn.* Garden City, N.Y., 1961.

YANESH, LEO. "The Campaign of 1812," in *Rewriting Russian History,* ed. CYRIL E. BLACK. New York, 1956.

III. THE CONTEMPORARY EXPERIENCE

General Works

BALCOS, ANASTASE. "Guerrilla Warfare," *Military Review,* XXXVII (March, 1958).

BJELAJAC, SLAVKO N. "Unconventional Warfare in the Nuclear Era," *Orbis,* IV (Fall, 1960).

BRYGOO, R. "Les Armées nationales et la difficile mission du maintien de l'ordre," *Revue Militaire Générale,* January, 1960.

CAVAGNES. "Les Opérations de maintien de l'ordre," *Revue Militaire Générale,* July, 1960.

CHASSIN, L. M. "Technique de l'insurrection," *Revue de Défense Nationale,* XIII (May, 1957).

CRIBEILLET, PAUL. *Vie et combats des partisans.* Paris, 1947.

CROZIER, BRIAN. *The Rebels.* Boston, 1960.

DELMAS, CLAUDE. *La guerre révolutionnaire.* Paris, 1959.

GLEASON, FRANK A. "Unconventional Forces: The Commander's Untapped Resources," *Military Review,* XXXIX (October, 1959).

HEILBRUNN, OTTO. *Partisan Warfare*. New York, 1962.

HILSMAN, ROGER. "Internal War—The New Communist Tactic," *Military Review*, XLII (April, 1962).

HOGARD, J. "L'Armée française devant la guerre révolutionnaire," *Revue de Défense Nationale*, XIII (January, 1957).

———. "Guerre Révolutionnaire et pacification," *Revue Militaire d'Information*, January, 1957.

———. "Guerre Révolutionnaire ou révolution dans l'art de guerre," *Revue de Défense Nationale*, XII (December, 1956).

JOHNSON, CHALMERS A. "Civilian Loyalties and Guerrilla Conflict," *World Politics*, XIV, No. 4 (July, 1962).

KNORR, KLAUS. "Unconventional Warfare: Strategy and Tactics in Internal Political Strife," in *Unconventional Warfare*, ed. J. K. ZAWODNY (*The Annals of the American Academy of Political and Social Science*, Vol. CCCXLI), May, 1962.

KVEDER, D. "Territorial War: The New Concept of Resistance," *Military Review*, XXXIV (July, 1954).

LINDSAY, FRANKLIN A. "Unconventional Warfare," *Foreign Affairs*, XL (January, 1962).

MARTIN. "Guérilla, guerre en surface, guerre révolutionnaire," *Revue Militaire d'Information*, August, September, 1957.

MIKSCHE, F. O. *The Failure of Atomic Strategy*. New York, 1959.

———. *Secret Forces*. London, 1950.

NEMO, J. M. "The Place of Guerrilla Action in War," *Military Review*, XXXVII (November, 1957).

NEY, VIRGIL. "Guerrilla War and Modern Strategy," *Orbis,* II (Spring, 1958).

―――. *Notes on Guerrilla War: Principles and Practices.* Washington, D.C., 1961.

OSANKA, F. MARK (ed.). *Modern Guerrilla Warfare.* New York, 1962.

A collection of previously published articles, with an Introduction by Samuel P. Huntington.

PAPAGOS, ALEXANDER. "Guerrilla Warfare," *Foreign Affairs,* XXX (January, 1952).

PARET, PETER. "The French Army and la Guerre Révolutionnaire," *Journal of the Royal United Service Institution,* CIV (February, 1959); reprinted in *Survival,* I (March–April, 1959).

―――. "A Total Weapon of Limited War," *Journal of the Royal United Service Institution,* CV (February, 1960).

PERRET-GENTIL, J. "L'Armée française face à la guerre subversive," *L'Armée–La Nation,* XIII (October, November, December, 1959) and XV (May, 1960).

ROLLAND, PIERRE. *Contre-Guérilla.* Paris, 1956.

ROSTOW, W. W. "Guerrilla Warfare in the Underdeveloped Areas," *The Department of State Bulletin,* No. 45 (August 7, 1961); reprinted in *The Guerrilla —And How to Fight Him: Selections from the* Marine Corps Gazette, ed. LIEUTENANT COLONEL T. N. GREENE. New York, 1962.

SOUYRIS, A. "Un Procédé efficace de contre-guérilla: l'auto-défense des populations," *Revue de Défense Nationale,* XII (June, 1956).

U.S. ARMY, SPECIAL WARFARE SCHOOL. *Readings in Guerrilla Warfare.* Fort Bragg, N.C., 1960.

VAN DE VELDE, ROBERT W. "The Neglected Deterrent," *Military Review,* XXXVIII (August, 1958).

"XIMENÈS," SOUYRIS, A., *et al.* "La Guerre révolutionnaire," *Revue Militaire d'Information,* February–March, 1957.

ZAWODNY, J. K. (ed.). *Unconventional Warfare (The Annals of the American Academy of Political and Social Science,* Vol. CCCXLI), May, 1962.

World War I

HOLT, EDGAR. *Protest in Arms: The Irish Troubles, 1916–1923.* New York, 1961.

LAWRENCE, T. E. "The Evolution of a Revolt," *The Army Quarterly,* XLI (October, 1920); reprinted in T. E. LAWRENCE, *Oriental Assembly.* London, 1939.

―――. *Seven Pillars of Wisdom.* New York, 1936.

The Russian Revolution

DINFREVILLE, JACQUES. "La Guerre de partisans dans le *Docteur Jivago,*" *Revue de Défense Nationale,* XVI (January, 1960).

GUSEV, S. I *Lessons of Civil War.* Moscow, 1958.

LENIN, VLADIMIR I. *Collected Works.* Moscow and London, 1960–.

The most comprehensive English edition of Lenin's works is now in process of publication. Writings on insurrection, partisans, and related topics can be found in several of the volumes.

―――. "Partisan Warfare," *Orbis,* II (Summer, 1958).

―――. *Selected Works.* 2 vols. Moscow, 1947.

TROTSKY, LEON. *The History of the Russian Revolution.* Translated by MAX EASTMAN. Ann Arbor, Mich., 1957.

World War II

BATTAGLIA, ROBERTO. *The Story of the Italian Resistance.* London, 1957.

BEAMISH, JOHN. *Burma Drop.* London, 1958.

CODÓ, ENRIQUE M. "Guerrilla Warfare in the Ukraine," *Military Review,* XL (November, 1960).

CONDIT, D. M. *Case Study in Guerrilla War: Greece During World War II.* Washington, D.C., 1961.

DE GAULLE, CHARLES. *The War Memoirs of Charles de Gaulle.* 3 vols. New York, 1958–60.

DIXON, C. AUBREY, and HEILBRUNN, OTTO. *Communist Guerilla Warfare.* New York, 1954.

FIRST INTERNATIONAL CONFERENCE ON THE HISTORY OF THE RESISTANCE MOVEMENTS. *European Resistance Movements, 1939–45.* London, 1960.

HOWELL, EDGAR M. *The Soviet Partisan Movement, 1941–1944.* Washington, D.C., 1956.

KISSEL, HANS. "Der deutsche Volkssturm, 1944–1945," *Wehrwissenschaftliche Rundschau,* X (April, 1960).

KOVPAK, SIDOR O. *Our Partisan Course.* London, 1947.

LEVY, BERT. *Guerrilla Warfare.* New York, 1943.

LIDDELL HART, BASIL H. "Were we wise to foster 'Resistance Movements'?," *Defense of the West.* New York, 1950.

MACLEAN, FITZROY. *Disputed Barricade.* London, 1957.

OGBURN, CHARLTON. *The Marauders.* New York, 1959.

REDELIS, VALDIS. *Partisanenkrieg.* Heidelberg, 1958.

ROMANUS, CHARLES F., and SUNDERLAND, RILEY. *Stilwell's Command Problems*. Washington, D.C., 1956.

STALIN, JOSEPH. *Works,* VI. Moscow, 1954.

TAYLOR, J. G. "Air Support for Guerrillas on Cebu," *Military Affairs*, XXIII, No. 3 (Fall, 1959).

TESKE, H. "Partisanen gegen die Eisenbahn." *Wehrwissenschaftliche Rundschau*, III (October, 1953).

WOLFERT, IRA. *American Guerrilla in the Philippines*. New York, 1945.

The Far East

BEEBE, JOHN E. "Beating the Guerrillas in South Korea," *Military Review*, XXXV (December, 1955).

BONNET, GABRIEL. "Mao Tse-tung et la strategie révolutionnaire," *Revue de Défense Nationale*, XI (January, 1955).

BURCHETT, WILFRED. *North of the 17th Parallel*. Delhi, 1956.

CHIU, S. M. *Chinese Communist Revolutionary Strategy, 1945–1949: Extracts from Volume IV of Mao Tse-tung's Selected Works*. Research Monograph No. 13, Center of International Studies, Princeton University, 1961.

CRAWFORD, OLIVER. *The Door Marked Malaya*. London, 1958.

DEPARTMENT OF STATE. *A Threat to the Peace: North Viet-Nam's Effort to Conquer South Viet-Nam*. 2 vols. Washington, D.C., 1961.

FALL, BERNARD. *Street Without Joy*. Harrisburg, Pa., 1961.

HAMMER, K. M. "Huks in the Philippines," *Military Review*, XXXVI (April, 1956).

HANRAHAN, GENE Z. "The Chinese Red Army and Guerrilla Warfare," *U.S. Army Combat Forces Journal,* February, 1951.

JACOBS, WALTER D. "Mao Tse-tung as a Guerrilla: A Second Look," *Military Review,* XXXVII (February, 1958).

JONAS, ANNE M., and TANHAM, GEORGE K. "Laos: A Phase in Cyclic Regional Revolution," *Orbis,* V (Spring, 1961).

JORDAN, GEORGE B. "Objectives and Methods of Communist Guerrilla Warfare," *Military Review,* XXXIX (January, 1960).

KARNOW, STANLEY. "Diem Defeats His Own Best Troops," *The Reporter,* January 19, 1961.

KATZENBACH, EDWARD L., JR. "Indo-China: A Military-Political Appreciation," *World Politics,* IV (January, 1952).

————, and HANRAHAN, GENE Z. "The Revolutionary Strategy of Mao Tse-tung," *Political Science Quarterly,* LXX (September, 1955).

LIU, F. F. *A Military History of Modern China.* Princeton, N.J., 1956.

MAO TSE-TUNG. *Mao Tse-tung on Guerrilla Warfare.* Translated by BRIGADIER GENERAL SAMUEL B. GRIFFITH. New York, 1961.

————. *On the Protracted War.* Peking, 1954.

————. *Problems of War and Strategy.* Peking, 1954.

————. *The Selected Works of Mao Tse-tung.* 4 vols. London, 1954–56.

————. *Strategic Problems in the Anti-Japanese Guerrilla War.* Peking, 1960.

————. *Strategic Problems of China's Revolutionary War.* Peking, 1954.

MIERS, RICHARD. *Shoot to Kill.* London, 1959.
An account by a participant of antiguerrilla operations in Malaya.

NAIRN, R. C. "Counter-Guerrilla Warfare in Southeast Asia," in *The Revolution in World Politics,* ed. MORTON KAPLAN. New York, 1962.

PARET, PETER. "Power and Politics in Asia," *The New Leader,* April 30, 1962.

PYE, LUCIAN. *Guerrilla Communism in Malaya: Its Social and Political Meaning.* Princeton, N.J., 1956.

————. "Lessons from the Malayan Struggle Against Communism." Mimeographed. Communist Bloc Program Part 17, Center for International Studies, Massachusetts Institute of Technology, 1957.

————. "The Policy Implications of Social Change in Non-Western Societies." Mimeographed. Communist Bloc Program Part 18, Center for International Studies, Massachusetts Institute of Technology, 1957.

RIESSEN, RENÉ. *Jungle Mission.* New York, 1957.

ROGERS, LINDSAY. *Guerrilla Surgeon.* London, 1957.

SCAFF, ALVIN M. *The Philippine Answer to Communism.* Stanford, Calif., 1955.

T'ANG LEANG-LI (ed.). *Suppressing Communist Banditry in China.* Shanghai, 1934.

TANHAM, GEORGE K. *Communist Revolutionary Warfare: The Vietminh in Indochina.* New York, 1961.

TARUC, CORRIS. *Born of the People.* New York, 1953.

VO NGUYÊN GIAP. *La guerre de libération et l'armée populaire.* Hanoi, 1950.

————. *People's War, People's Army: The Viet Cong Insurrection Manual for Underdeveloped Countries.* With an Introduction by ROGER HILSMAN. New York, 1962.

WAN YAH-KANG. *The Rise of Communism in China— 1920–1950.* Hong Kong, 1952.

WANG HUO. *Chieh Chen-kuo, Guerrilla Hero.* Peking, 1961.

A Communist novel about guerrilla warfare.

YANG SHANG-KUEI. *The Red Kiangsi-Kwangtung Border Region.* Peking, 1961.

A Communist novel about guerrilla warfare.

Africa and the Near East

BEGIN, MENACHEM. *The Revolt.* London, 1951.

An account of Israeli operations in the 1940's.

BEHR, EDWARD. *The Algerian Problem.* New York, 1962.

BRAESTRUP, PETER. "Partisan Tactics—Algerian Style," *Army,* August, 1960.

CORFIELD, F. D. *Historical Survey of the Origins and Growth of Mau Mau.* London, 1960.

DÉON, MICHEL. *L'Armée d'Algerie et la pacification.* Paris, 1959.

DESJOURS, J. "La Pacification dans le secteur de Blida," *Revue des Forces Terrestres,* October, 1959.

LORCH, NETANEL. *The Edge of the Sword: Israel's War of Independence, 1947–1949.* New York, 1961.

NE'EMAN, YUVAL. "The Israeli Army and the Sinai Campaign," *Norsk Militaer Tidsskrift,* CXIX (December, 1960).

KITSON, FRANK. *Gangs and Counter-Gangs.* London, 1960.

An account by a participant of operations against the Mau Mau.

POIRIER, L. "Un Instrument de guerre révolutionnaire: le F. L. N.," *Revue Militaire d'Information,* January, 1958.

Europe

BARKER, DUDLEY. *Grivas, Portrait of a Terrorist.* London, 1959.

BAUMANN, GERHARD. "Der militärische Wert der SED-Kampfgruppen," *Wehrkunde,* VIII (October, 1959).

CHASSIN, L. M. "Révolte en Hongrie," *Revue de Défense Nationale,* XIII (June, 1957).

DACH BERN, H. v. *Der totale Widerstand: Kleinkriegsanleitung für jedermann.* Biel, 1958.

EITNER, HANS-JÜRGEN. "Die 'Kampfgruppen der SED'—die Bürgerkriegsmiliz der SBZ," *Wehrwissenschaftliche Rundschau,* X (June, 1960).

PAPATHANASIADES, T. "The Bandits' Last Stand in Greece," *Military Review,* XXX (February, 1951).

ZACHARAKIS, E. E. "Lessons Learned from the Antiguerrilla War in Greece," *Revue Militaire Générale,* July, 1960.

The American Hemisphere

Army, XII, No. 8 (March, 1962).
Contains policy statements and articles on guerrilla warfare.

DRAPER, THEODORE. "Cubans and Americans," *Encounter,* XVII (July, 1961).

GREENE, LIEUTENANT COLONEL T. N. (ed.). *The Guer-*

rilla—And How to Fight Him: Selections from the Marine Corps Gazette. New York, 1962.

GUEVARA, ERNESTO. *Che Guevara on Guerrilla Warfare.* With an Introduction by MAJOR HARRIES-CLICHY PETERSON. New York, 1961.

HAUPT, WERNER. "Der Partisanenkrieg auf Cuba," *Wehrwissenschaftliche Rundschau,* IX (February, 1959).

Marine Corps Gazette. Special Issue: Guerrilla Warfare, XLVI, No. 1 (January, 1962).

PARET, PETER, and SHY, JOHN W. "Guerrilla Warfare and U.S. Military Policy: A Study," *Marine Corps Gazette,* XLVI, No. 1 (January, 1962); reprinted in *Survival,* IV (January–February, 1962); *The Airman,* May, 1962; *The Guerrilla—And How to Fight Him: Selections from the* Marine Corps Gazette, ed. LIEUTENANT COLONEL T. N. GREENE. New York, 1962.

U.S. ARMY. *Field Manual 41–10: Civil Affairs Operations.* [Final Manuscript Draft.] Washington, D.C., December, 1961.

————. *Field Manual 100–1: Doctrinal Guidance.* Washington, D.C., September, 1959.

————. *Field Manual 31–21: Guerrilla Warfare and Special Forces Operations.* Washington, D.C., May, 1958.

————. *Field Manual 31–21: Guerrilla Warfare and Special Operations.* Washington, D.C., September, 1961.

————. *Field Manual 31–15: Operations Against Irregular Forces.* Washington, D.C., May, 1961.